Name Your Pet

D0957985

Name Your Pet

*the easy way to solve
an agonising problem
that afflicts nearly
every normal family,
sooner or later . . .*

Alix Palmer
and
Robert Coole

inspired and assisted
by Daisy Coole

BLAKE

Published by Blake Publishing Ltd,
3 Bramber Court, 2 Bramber Road, London, England W14 9PB

First published in Great Britain in 1995

ISBN 1 85782 041X

British Library Cataloguing-in-Publication Data:
A catalogue record for this book is available from the British Library.

Typeset by CentraCet, Cambridge

Printed in Finland by WSOY

1 3 5 7 9 10 8 6 4 2

Contents

Foreword

The struggle had gone on for days and looked like lasting for weeks more. Family, friends, neighbours, schoolmates had all been consulted and all made suggestions, some less silly than others.

The subject of all this fuss? A ten-week-old Rough Collie – and what to call her. The pedigree certificate was awash with exotic names. But who'd really want to bellow: 'Heel, Pelido Hot Chocolate!' 'Sit, Snugborough Enuff!' 'Drop that, Cathanbrae Bon Ami of Sandridge!' 'Fetch, Sylps Truly Scrumptious!'

Because she's the breed made famous by the 'Lassie' films, half the world was urging us to be really boring and call her just that. We hit on something utterly different. And now she is Cassie – or, to the Kennel Club, Sylps Cassandra R04.

So far, so good. But then along came a new kitten. And then the extra puppy . . .

'Listen,' said the youngest in the family. 'I'm tired of trying to think up names for all these animals. They have books of names for babies – why can't they do one for pets?'

Very true, Daisy. So here it is . . .

How It Works

In theory, one list of names ought to do for both dogs and cats – and gerbils, goldfish and stick insects, if it comes to that. But there are names you would never call a dog (the possible embarrassment when you have to shout out a really silly one, aside). And on the whole, to make a cat come running, you either tweet or rattle a spoon on a dish. At the sound of the dinnergong, which a cat learns with its free ear even while taking the first slurp of mother's milk, few moggies will wait till you've announced their names properly. They're proud, but not *that* proud. So when naming a cat or kitten, you can really indulge yourself.

We have compiled a major A–Z list of names:

some we feel are mainly more doggy, some mainly for felines, others would happily do for dog *or* cat. It's all utterly arbitrary, and the result of research, deep thought, personal prejudice and (we hope) common sense.

You may notice that we tend to dwell on individual breeds in dogs much more than with cats. This is because we felt that far more people own a recognisable breed of dog than is the case with cats. And – apart from their engaging, fascinating habits as individuals – cats, as breeds, near-breeds or nowhere-near-breeds, seem to us to be more like other cats than dogs – except in the most basic ways – are like other dogs. Cats are much more of a race apart. And before you write in anger, take note that our family now has 350 per cent more cats than dogs!

As extra guides, we list the Top Ten pet names in Britain and the United States. Plus names of some famous screen pets, the pets of some famous people, including of course Royals. Plus the kind of names that kids come up with.

Now settle in for a highly informative read. But don't get so absorbed that you forget to take the dog out and let the cat in.

A-Z

*of Names for Dogs,
Cats, Hims and Hers*

A

Mainly for Dogs

If It's a Him . . .

ADAM – from the Hebrew word for 'red'. Just right for a doughty, four-square pet, such as a Bulldog, Pug or Clumber Spaniel.

ALBERT – from the German for 'noble and bright'. Imported as a man's name, evidently, by the late Queen Victoria, in the person of her much-mourned Teutonic husband. Would suit a particularly dopey Labrador, or droopy Basset Hound with a keen sense of duty.

ANDREW – Greek for 'manly' and has the

advantage (you may think) of being the name of Her Britannic Majesty's second son. With this strongly in mind, maybe not the label to give a particularly bright, intelligent pet. More for a fearless, tail-wagging dumbo.

AUBREY – Norman French, this time. It meant 'Elf Ruler'. Nowadays you don't come across that many Aubreys. To us the name conjures up the picture of a salon smoothie. Try it for size on either a very large dog or a very, very small boudoir model.

If It's a Her . . .

ADA – from Old German for 'noble'. Best suited to a below-stairs kind of dog. See what she looks like in a maid's mob cap, before deciding.

AGGIE – from Agnes, Greek word meaning 'pure'. An easy one to shout out in the park. Bit of an imposition to put on any of the more dignified breeds, though.

ALEXANDRA – name favoured in European

Royal circles, so if you're that way inclined, or your pet has a streak of nobility about her, this would do a treat. (Always remember the golden rule: long name plus short legs equals big guffaw.)

ALMA – from Latin for 'loving'. Just right for a dog whose owner is one of that little cult of the long-gone pop singer Alma Cogan.

AMANDA – from Latin, 'worth loving'. Another of those glamour names. Don't take it on unless yours is a truly top-drawer dog, a real lady. On a cat, the name sounds a bit diamante.

AMY – from French Aimée. Which would cover just about any size, shape, breed and fluffiness of dog. If you've fallen for some pooch at first sight, remember the old song: *Once in love with Amy, always in love with Amy . . .*

ARABELLA – old Scots name. Would sound all right for a whole range of breeds. Fits an Afghan or Saluki as to the castle born, ideal for a haughty little Pekinese, would confer a little dignity on a comic-faced Dandie Din-mont. Any cat would be happy with such a handle: cats have so much more natural dignity than dogs.

ARIADNE – Greek, means 'most holy one'. Unless it's another of those three-in-the-morning thoughts, this one still seems to keep us in the big, grand dog territory. For a cat, probably a bit over-ripe.

Mainly for Cats

If It's a Him . . .

ALGERNON – invented as a nickname and perhaps best left as one, with its overtones of Burlington Bertie pretension. You wouldn't call your son Algernon, would you? So why get people laughing at your cat. Oh, what the hell . . . deep down, they're *all* Algernons. Anyway, there's always Algy.

AUBERON – *(see OBERON)*.

If It's a Her . . .

ABIGAIL – has had an up-and-down social life. The biggest up was when King David of the Israelites had a wife of this name. Hundreds of years on, in England, an 'Abigail' was what you called a humble maid. So the name was firmly struck off the list of possibles in any genteel home. These days, Abigail is again an OK name for humans – and very suitable for the more queenly kind of cat.

AMBER – a precious stone and, decades ago, the heroine of a racy (for its times) novel called *Forever Amber*. If you prefer the unusual, and your pet is not too much of a scruff, this could be a gem.

ARAMINTA – in Greek, 'defender'. Has much the same feel to it as Arabella – even more rarefied, if anything. Can shorten to Minty, if that's any help with your choice.

ATALANTA – a Princess of ancient Greek myth, daughter of King Minos of Crete, who vowed to wed only a man who could run faster than her. Just when she thought it was safe to put away the running spikes, along came this chap Milanion, with a wedding challenge. A disdainful Atalanta had to accept. And the cad actually won – by dropping three golden apples behind him to slow her down. If you suspect your pet is faster than most, Atalanta is a most imposing name for her.

AYESHA – Arabic for 'womanly'. A truly feline, fruitily feminine name. But be choosy: on a fat old beaten-up alley cat, it would be ridiculous. Cats aren't daft, you know. She'd sooner leave home than answer to it.

Names for Dog *or* Cat

ALICE – from old German, meaning (as so many of these names do) 'noble'. Would suit a very feminine-looking pet with long, Alice-Through-the-Looking-Glass tresses. Afghan Hound, perhaps, or Shih-Tzu. Or a very sedate cat.

AMBROSE – name of an eminent early-Christian scholar. Another for the Basset Hound, perhaps?

AMOS – prophet of doom in the Old Testament. Suits the kind of dog who hides in a cupboard six hours before the thunder and lightning becomes obvious to the rest of us. Or a cat that sits and stares a lot.

ANNA – variant of Ann, which comes from Hannah, which in Bible times meant 'God's favourite'. For the naughty-but-nice little pet, try Annie.

ANTIGONE – pronounced, of course, An-tig-onee. She was the daughter of old King Oedipus, who had troubles of his own, and she was a bit too full of herself. She went around claiming to be just as beautiful as those enticing nymphs of the Aegean Sea, the Nereids. Well, they weren't having that, and she ended up chained to a rock, the pudding course for a sea monster's free lunch. Luckily, along came Perseus to rescue her. Meeting in such circumstances, of course, they were obliged to get wed, and did. What's all that got to do

9

with your new pet, do you ask? Well, it's a jolly impressive, elegant name, one for Puss to be proud of.

ARCHIBALD – in German, once meant 'truly bold'. The kind of name that might sound hilarious over the fifth bottle of christening Californian red at three in the morning. In which case, have a further discussion next day, sober. As for a cat, it might sound cute. But it is a bit ... well, *arch*. Archie, on the other hand, really suits lots of either species.

AUGUSTUS – Latin for 'majesty'. You could certainly name your big Dalmatian Augustus – or any other breed that can stand the imperious weight of it. Since there is no chance of the name not being shortened to Gus or Gussie, consider whether that version would still suit.

B

Mainly for Dogs

If It's a Him . . .

BALDRIC – from the German meaning 'bold'. Specially appealing, perhaps, to fans of British TV's anarcho-comic 'Blackadder' series, with the hero's smelly, unwashed accomplice, Baldric. But if a prospective pet looks like suiting the name, maybe he's not quite right for your nice polished, lavender-scented little nest.

BARRY – we'd have said OK for a human, deeply boring on a dog. But if there's some rich old Uncle Barry you want to suck up to (or take a rise out of) go ahead. We can't say it suits any particular breed. It really is *that* boring!

BASIL – Greek for 'king-like'. Despite its posh antecedents, hardly a name to bellow in the park, is it? But if it amuses you that much, try it out on a lovable Basset, which has the mournful dignity to carry it off, however reproachfully. Or a Dachshund or Jack Russell, neither of which could acquire dignity even if the vet gave it to them by hypodermic.

BEN/BENNY – Biblical Benjamin was Jacob's youngest son (of twelve), and the family pet. Ben is right for just about any faithful, easy-to-please breed - especially perhaps Beagle or Boxer. Or any mongrel with floppy ears and the urge to roll over and be tickled.

BERT – like Fred (*which also see*), one of those affectedly downmarket names often favoured by our social superiors, to get even with the masses. From the German Bertram, meaning (for whatever weighty Teutonic reason) 'bright raven'. Bertram might make an alternative to Basil, if you're that desperate.

BILL/BILLY – the diminutive, as we all know, of William (*which also see*). Bill is bound to remind some people of the celebrated Dickens burglar, Bill Sikes, and *his* rough, tough dog. For a Bull, Pit Bull or Staffordshire Bull Terrier. Billy, of course, is altogether more carefree: an English Setter, perhaps? Or more likely, Animal Shelter Inmate No. 23456Y?

BOB/BOBBY – diminutive of Robert, naturally. From German meaning 'bright renown'. Bob, perhaps, for a no-nonsense, no-special-kind dog who knows his own way back from the pub. Bobby, if he's little and lovable: a Yorkie, Cairn. (*See also* BOBBIE.)

BRETT – from Breton (Briton, or native of Brittany, France). Smacks of back-lot cowboys and Aussie soaps. If you can put up with the giggles, all right for a poser's dog (American Pit Bull, or – in the city where he doesn't belong – Great Dane).

If It's a Her . . .

BABETTE – version of Barbara, martyred patron saint of artillerymen. You'd only do this to a real boudoir beauty: Pekinese, Chihuahua, toy Poodle, miniature Schnauzer.

BELLA – spin-off from Belinda (*see Cats*). Bestow it either on an utterly beautiful creature (Small Continental Spaniel, Papillon, Afghan Hound) or a dumpy *hausfrau* (Clumber Spaniel, Labrador).

BLODWEN – from Welsh 'white flower'. It's so much a Land of My Fathers name, you could only sensibly give it to a Welsh Terrier, Springer Spaniel – or, most likely, to a Corgi.

BOBBIE – feminised version of Bobby, and for much the same kind of personality.

BONNIE – could suit a pet who, as the Scots say, is bonny, meaning fine or attractive. If she's a bit of a tearaway, remember the notorious gangster duo, Bonnie and Clyde.

Mainly for Cats

If It's a Him . . .

BAMBI – after the Disney deer-baby, of course (*see Screen Stars*). Which suggests a cat with extra-large, extra-round, extra-wondering eyes, such as a British Blue. (Away from Disneyland, a human Bambi is more likely to be a Her, so anything goes.)

If It's a Her . . .

BATHSHEBA – another one from Biblical times, meaning 'voluptuous'. The original Bathsheba was voluptuous enough for King David of the Hittites to get her husband, Uriah, killed in battle – and grab her for himself. Most apt for a truly glamorous, pure-bred Abyssinian.

BELINDA – signifies wisdom. Since all cats look wise (or at the very least, cunning: just see one crouched over a stolen chicken bone), you could call pretty well any moggie Belinda. Perhaps a bit posh for the one-eared alley cat, though there's no harm trying to boost her morale a little.

Names for Dog *or* Cat

BARTHOLOMEW – from the Hebrew, to do with furrows, for some far-fetched reason. So it's absolutely spot-on for a super-wrinkly Shar-pei, or Chinese Fighting Dog. Otherwise, though superficially imposing, it could be a bit twee. But anyway, there would a a swift and certain slide into Bart or Barty.

BERTHA – nicely old-fashioned name, from old German for 'bright'. Those wishing to display a sense of history might choose it in allusion to Big Bertha, the famous German artillery giant of World War One, but only if you've got the right-size dog – an Akita, say, or Tosa. Or if it looks really pugnacious, like the British Bulldog. If a cat, Bertha goes nicely with the home-loving fireside model.

BORIS – splendidly dignified name. Would suit a muscle-man Mastiff or, if he's a bit of fun, a tiny Pomeranian or Chihuaha. Your Boris cat would be a heavyweight, with always first choice of armchairs.

BRANDY – if the colour is right, this name is as good as any. Some people might think it a bit obvious for a Cognac-coloured pet. We'd prefer to say *popular*. Bestow this name on a Him or a Her.

C

Mainly for Dogs

If It's a Him . . .

CAMERON – for a dashing West Highland White Terrier, but since they're notoriously sensitive little souls, don't mention the original Gaelic meaning: 'wonky nose'.

CERBERUS – in Greek myth, he was a three-headed dog who sat guarding the gates of Hell. Without counting heads, this sounds ideal for a Bulldog.

CHARLES – very, very distinguished old name indeed. From Germany via Rome via France.

Apart from a King Charles Spaniel, which might seem a bit obvious, this would nicely suit a whole range of breeds. If your pet is a comic turn, he'll be Charlie, as in Chaplin, won't he?

CHUMLEIGH/CHUMLEY/CHOLMONDE-LEY – one of the good old English aristo-name jokes. If it sounds fun, it will need an uncomplaining sort of dog. Which means it might suit a non-barking, happy-go-lucky Basenji.

CRISPIN – from Latin for 'curly'. Which surely points us in the direction of the wondrously wavy English Toy Spaniel, or any unshaven Poodle or Kerry Blue Terrier. Decisive-sounding name for when you're giving the orders.

CRITTER – as in 'pore dumb critter' from all those Western movies. Recommendation: take it or leave it. After all, it's your dog . . .

If It's a Her . . .

CANDICE – from old-time Ethiopia's Royal line. Hard to stop vulgar people shortening it to Candy, of course. The full-length version, though, would suit a frou-frou little dog-ette: Papillon, King Charles Spaniel, Maltese, Dandie Dinmont.

CARA – from the Italian for 'dear one'. Pretty much a general-purpose sort of name. Either you go for it, or you don't.

CHARITY – means what it says, and if you get your little beauty from the animal shelter, what better name than this? If it's a three-legged, one-eyed mangy mongrel, though, do think again: you really shouldn't rub it in.

Mainly for Cats

If It's a Him . . .

CEDRIC – sounds very ancient Anglo-Saxon, but was evidently an instant invention of the nineteenth-century novelist Sir Walter Scott. Would suit a cheeky-chappie type of cat (or perhaps fairly imposing dog).

CLARENCE – male version of Clare, from the Irish county name. A Duke of Clarence was among the hotly tipped candidates for Jack the Ripper.

If It's a Her . . .

CANDIDA – from ancient Rome, meaning 'white'. Reserved for the grander class of pet, we feel.

CAROLINE – one of the feminine variations on Charles.

CIRCE – mythical Greek enchantress who turned the long-ranging Ulysses' shipmates to real swine. Some trick. Just find your enchantress . . .

CLARE/CLARRY – (see CLARENCE). We wouldn't choose Clare as a pet's name, but Clarry would suit a lovable mog of no particular breed, class or colour.

CRYSTAL – all cats, of course, are by nature clean. If you have a pure white Persian, take a chance on her ability to stay that way, and plunge on this one.

Names for Dogs *or* Cats

CALYPSO – forget the first thought that springs to mind. She was the Greek nymph who, one way or another, managed to delay that famous master mariner, Ulysses, for seven years on his way home from Troy. We bet he told the missus it was all his shipmates' fault. Another enchantress, obviously (*see CIRCE*).

CASSANDRA – she was a princess in ancient Troy and one of the god Apollo's priestesses. Bound to shorten to Cassie, which at least is easy to hiss. If you give this name to a Lassie-type Rough Collie, be prepared for tiresome mishearings by friends and neighbours. In its full-out version, ideal for a biggish, sleek dog such as a Setter or Dalmatian, or a similarly slinky cat.

CHLOE – an alternative name for the Greek goddess of fertility, Demeter. Probably more for a cat than a dog, though it might be all right for, say, a miniature Dachshund.

D

Mainly for Dogs

If It's a Him . . .

DAFFY – for that rush-around, tear-it-up,
happy-yappy pup who's never going to
calm down, but makes up for all the uproar
with tremendous affection. English Setter,
Dalmatian.

DALE – as in up hill, down dale. Originally
meant 'someone who dwells in the dale'.
Probably best for a big, tough specimen:
German Shepherd, Rottweiler, Doberman.

DALEY – as in D. Thompson, our greatest

athlete. If you've got an Alsatian/German Shepherd who can take an 80 m.p.h. run-up over a 15-foot wall, what better, prouder title than this?

DANA – since it means 'a Dane', why look further to name your Great D?

DANIEL – if you've got the kind of dog who'd brave a lions' den (or at least, a burglar's Doc Martens) here's a suitably bold and dignified name for him. Danny, of course, if he's one of the Irish breeds: Wolfhound, for example. Note: a courageous Daniel doesn't have to be big.

DARIUS – ancient Persian for defender. Not too embarrassing to have to howl out of the back door.

DARREN – nobody quite knows where it comes from, and it's the kind of nothing name you'd expect somebody with tattoos behind the ears to bestow on his best motorbike. Or Pit Bull. Our recommendation: if you can actually read this, skip Darren.

DAVID – well, he slew Goliath and was made King of Israel, so he must have had something. On a human, a decent, dependable name. For a dog, Davy seems more likely – especially for a lovable mongrel.

DEAN – from old English 'dweller in the valley', but we bet there's more of the suicide-heroic James Dean tendency here: a kamikaze Rotty or Shih-tzu. Or, heaven help us, Dean *Martin*? In which case, we beg to pass. And so, as likely as not, will your dignified dog.

DEL – well. It used to be short for such names as Delbert. Nowadays, a slack-jawed distortion of Derek. We'd expect to find Del Dog tied by a bootlace alongside some canal, waiting for its owner to come home from Parkhurst. But you never know . . .

DEMETRIUS – another Greek god-follower, this time the earth-mother goddess Demeter, who looked after the farmers. Clumber Spaniel, English/Irish Setter, Great Dane, Mastiff.

DENIS – from Greek Dionysius, meaning a

worshipper of the god of wine and poetry. Nowadays, a homely name for a homely dog: a chubby mongrel with a bit of Labrador, perhaps.

DENZIL – strong-sounding, romantic name with a Cornish background. Would suit a Cornish breed, if there were any. Good for a Boxer, Mastiff, Great Dane.

DERMOT – after a great lover in Irish myth (and around a dozen saints). Any kind of dog, if he meets the right girl.

DONALD – these days people are likely to think either of Duck or Donald, Where's Yer Troosis? Yet this Celtic name started out as a highly noble one, meaning mighty. Since your pet can scarcely trot along with an explanatory placard round his neck, if you go for Donald, make sure you choose a comical dog – a Cairn or smooth-haired Dachshund.

DOPEY – remembering this is one of Snow White's Seven Dwarfs, this could also do for a Dachshund, though the name would belie his very sharp intelligence.

DUKE – from the Welsh for lucky. Rather vulgar for a big German Shepherd or Doberman. Think of it, perhaps, for one of the small, exquisite pets, such as Maltese.

If It's a Her . . .

DAHLIA – a flower name that has become a bit of a joke, thanks to P.G. Wodehouse's Aunt Dahlia character. Restore its rightful dignity by giving it, perhaps, to a high-speed Whippet or courageous Irish Terrier.

DALLAS – Wild West saloon name for the flirty type who's free with her affections: a Golden Retriever?

DELIA – a name much favoured by ancient Latin love poets. Suits a proud beauty: Afghan, Saluki, Borzoi.

DILLY – from the Welsh Dilys, which means

'genuine'. One for an honest little dog, such as a Jack Russell.

DOLLY – a form of Dorothy which would really suit a clown dog, such as the merry, lovable Cairn or West Highland White.

DONNA – if you'd really like to call your pet Lady, but don't want to join the thousands of others who have already done it (*see Your Top Ten Names for Pets*), this Italian version of the word may appeal. For the dignified Bichon or Afghan.

Mainly for Cats

If It's a Him . . .

DIM-SUM – tasty name for an Oriental-looking pet, straight off the Chinese takeaway menu.

DO-DO – if he's not too bright, but specially cuddly and fond of human laps.

DUM-DUM – for the cat that never seems to find his food first time.

If It's a Her . . .

DEE-DEE – an affectionate variation on Diana, Dorothy or Deirdre/Deidre.

DESIREE – from the French, it would mean 'the pet we've been longing to have'.

DONATA – from Latin, meaning 'a gift'. Need we say more?

Names for Dog *or* Cat

DAFFODIL – a pretty flower-name that a chap might not want to bellow across a crowded park. Otherwise, it could be right for a dopey-looking Labrador or an elegant Lurcher. Ideal for a specially pretty cat.

DAISY – from Day's Eye, one of the many variants of the seemingly unconnected Marguerite/Margaret. Slightly twee for a really tiny or pretty dog, but OK for, say, a Great Dane (which can stand it) or Greyhound (which can outrun it).

DERVLA – charmingly Irish, but you'll have to keep spelling it for people. It means 'desire'.

DINAH – quite a sweet name. Until you peek at the Bible story of a famous Dinah of ancient times, whose beauty caused quite a bit of bother. This Dinah, daughter of Jacob and Leah, was kidnapped by a chap named Schechem, who fell in love and wanted to marry her. His father, Hamer, put in a word with Jacob's family and it was agreed that Hamer and all his male relatives should be circumcised, like Dinah's lot. In return, there would be a big inter-tribal mass wedding. But while Hamer and his men were getting over the operation, Dinah's two brothers crept into their city, slaughtered all the men and made off with their sister, all the oxen, all the asses and all the sheep. *If you get a pup who chews a slipper too far, Dinah should suit her very well* . . .

DIRK – variation on Derek, and a lot more dashing it is, too. For a devil-may-care dog, or dashing cat-about-tiles.

DO-DO – from Dorothy, suits a slipper-loving pooch as well as a fireside cat.

DULCIE – from Latin for 'sweet'.

E

Mainly for Dogs

If It's a Him . . .

EAMONN – variation of Edmond (*see below*).

EDGAR – from Old English, roughly meaning 'lucky spear'. Right for an Eager Edgar dog: a West Highland White?

EDWIN – another Old English name which means 'lucky friend'. Not a specially doggy name, but would suit a loyal English Bulldog.

EGBERT – Old English, carrying suggestions of high intelligence. Rough Collie, Clumber

Spaniel, Newfoundland, Bedlington or Boston Terrier.

ELMER – if you're a Bugs Bunny fan with a cartwheeling Cairn, look no further.

EMLYN – strictly for the rugger-size animal. Rottweiler, Tosa, Akita – but especially a Boxer.

ERIC – though sounding rather soppy these days, it's a Viking name. So we're in fierce-fighter territory. American Pit Bull, Staffordshire Bull, Rottweiler, Doberman. Shortens to Rick/Ricky.

EUGENE – from Greek word that means 'well-bred'. Several saints have borne the name: not that we expect many saints in the doggie world. Just right for an upstanding Great Dane or Newfoundland. The feminine version, Eugenie, was of course favoured by the Duchess of York for one of her daughters.

EUSTACE – there was a medieval St Eustace. And a British tabloid newspaper for decades ran a cartoon spot called Useless Eustace. One to consider, if he's a hopeless sort of animal.

EZEKIEL – name of a Bible prophet. Shortens, of course, to Zeke.

Mainly for Cats

If It's a Him . . .

EBENEZER – Biblical, with an origin, to do with a celebrated Israelite victory, that doesn't help much when it comes to deciding whether to bestow it on your pet. Seems to us to need a really wise-looking animal.

EBONY – a little obvious for a sleek black beauty, perhaps, but satisfyingly suitable. Comes from the smooth black wood of the ebony tree. Perfectly OK for a lady cat, too.

EDWARD – as with Andrew, one of those Royal names to choose or avoid, depending whether you're a monarchist or not. Despite some flamboyant exceptions, choose this for a

Steady Eddie type of pet: a teddy-bear style of puss.

EMANUEL – for the more imperious kind. After all, the name, in Hebrew, does mean 'God With Us'. For a rather saucy female, Emanuelle is exotic.

If It's a Her . . .

ELEANOR – ancient name with many suggested origins, none of them much to do with the others. Elegant for a queenly cat.

ELSPETH – another version of Elizabeth. Take your pick.

ELVIRA – from Spanish, with artistic connections. In Noël Coward's play, *Blithe Spirit*, Elvira was the enchanting ghost of a first wife who still kept her claws on hubby.

ERASMUS – in Greek, it means 'beloved'. Would sound affected on a dog, but suits a particularly educated-looking cat.

35

ESMERALDA – Spanish for 'emerald'. For a jewel-like beauty or a rag-tailed scruff in need of a morale-lift.

Names for Dog *or* Cat

ELIZABETH – for the dog with Elizabeth Taylor beauty (Irish Setter, or Shih-tzu/Yorkie in full evening dress). For a cat, though, better if she's the homely cottage style.

ELLA – short form of Eleanor. Splendid for a big dog or small. Equally suited to the prouder kind of cat.

ELTON – rock fans need no explanation or guidance: your pet is a flamboyant, entertaining E. John type or he isn't. But check a picture book of dogs to make sure your scatty pup won't grow into a stuffy old fogey.

ELVIS – well, there's only the one, isn't there? If you're a Presley fan, nothing on this earth (or under it) is going to stop you giving your hero's name to your unsuspecting dog or cat, especially an obsessive yowler. And in the dog world, there's no better yowler than the Tibetan Terrier, whose bark is more like an air-raid siren.

EMILY – ancient Rome family name. For a prim armchair dog or cosy, window-watching cat.

EMMA – rather more dog than cat, we feel, on balance. Used in this country for getting on a thousand years, and today more popular than ever, for human girls. Think of it for an aristocratic Sealyham Terrier, or cuddly cat.

ENA – older pet lovers will think instantly of old Ena Sharples, way back in the mists of TV's 'Coronation Street'. But it doesn't have to be a stout-and-hairnet kind of name. There was a Princess Ena, daughter of Queen Victoria, who became the Queen of Spain. So there! Would your pet be happy as Ena? Only you can work it out.

ENOCH – he was Adam's descendant (aren't we all?) who got on specially well with God, lived 365 years and arrived in Heaven without being put to the bother of dying first. For the pet who always seems to be under your feet.

ETHEL – vaguely Old English for 'noble'. Nowadays, for a below-stairs comic type, whether dog or cat.

ETHELBERT – variation of Albert. Bound to be cut down to Bert, though not, we hope, to Ethel.

EVE/EVA/EVIE – for the homely, Earth Mother type of pet. She can also be Evelyn.

F

Mainly for Dogs

If It's a Him . . .

FERDINAND – part-Spanish name that generally denotes bravery, even though it was given to the cartoon little bull who just hated the idea of fighting. Seems very suited to a little dog with a big, bold personality. There are plenty of those, but we'd certainly include Chihuahua, Shih-tzu, Yorkie.

If It's a Her . . .

FAWN – for that eager, anxious-eyed pet, or any dog who's a suitable colour, as long as she's gentle (*see BAMBI*). Unkind to use in its other sense, if your pup turns out to be a fawning, over-eager pet.

FLORRIE – from Florence, of course, which is somehow rather stilted for a dog, while Florrie would be an excellent choice if your pet is a bit common, but lovable with it. Specially for a dogs' home dog.

Mainly for Cats

If It's a Him . . .

FRANCIS – started with the Franks, a German horde who went on the rampage across Europe 1,500 years ago and gave France its present name. Your cat, like most, will probably be graciously inclined to take over any seat, bed or tabletop you were about to use yourself. On that ground alone, consider Francis. There is also Frankie. (*See also FRANCES.*)

If It's a Her . . .

FAITH – for the kind of cat who still wants to

be on your lap, even after she's been well fed, and even though she could have chosen the deep-pile carpet in front of a blazing log fire. Possibly not much call for Faith, as a cat name!

FAY – (*see FAITH*).

FENELLA – another one from the Celtic, with no particular meaning, but a superior county-girl sound to it. Best for a cat who's lean, clean and slightly mean.

FRANCES – is of course the feminine form of Francis, though it seems to suit someone more ladylike than a Frankish flibbertygibbet. For the well-settled, domestic puss-about-the-kitchen.

Names for Dog *or* Cat

FELIX – male version of Felicity, once famous as a 1920s movie cartoon character ('Felix Kept on Walking'). There seems no reason why you shouldn't call a dog Felix: either because he's permanently happy, or because he's one of those mournful pooches who always looks at you as if he's just missed his daily walk.

FERGUS – old Celtic meaning 'energetic one'. Obviously right for an Irish breed of dog: Setter, Terrier, Wolfhound. Or for a robust, short-haired, extra-independent cat.

FLAVIA – wow! She'll need to look the super-aristocrat carry off this one. Flavia stems from the family name of Roman Emperors, no less. And of course was grand enough for a Princess Flavia to be the heroine in that wonderful Ruritarian melodrama, *The Prisoner of Zenda*. (*see ZENDA*).

FLORA – it went out of fashion anyway, and became even more of a problem when the name was plastered all over a brand of margarine. But it's pretty, and Flora was Roman goddess of flowers and fertility. Piquant choice for a really puggish Bulldog, more obviously suitable for Golden Retriever or Labrador. As to cats, only the most beaten-up, smelly moggie fails to look as decorative as a bowl of flowers around the house, so it would suit pretty well any kind.

FLOWER – more likely to be given to a pony than a household pet, but, we think, prettier than the Latin Flora.

FREDA – (*see FREDERICK*).

FREDERICK/FREDRIC – from German, meaning 'peaceful ruler'. By the sound of it, would ideally suit a Border Collie: as herding dogs, they are reputed to be able to put a cow in a trance! Frederick will soon shorten to Fred or Freddie.

G

Mainly for Dogs

If It's a Him . . .

GENE – this abbreviation of the distinctive Eugene has got a bit shopworn at the vulgar end of showbiz. Goes best, if at all, with a sort-of German Shepherd, sort-of Doberman or sort-of Rottweiler.

GLENN – Celtic for 'valley'. Glam movie actress Glenn Close, and space explorer John Glenn, gave an uninspired name a bit of a lift. Oh yes, for the older set, there was also G. Miller, the swing-band leader. But still, we would say, this is a solid, stolid sort of name. Your Labrador would like it.

If It's a Her . . .

GAIL/GAYLE – from Abigail. Gail, obviously, as in TV's 'Coronation Street'. Gayle as in the supremely glamorous American actress Gayle Hunnicutt. Homely Gail would go with a comfy, unspectacular but affectionate dog of no particular breed. Spectacular Gayle: Afghan Hound, Silky Terrier.

GAYNOR – a twist on Jennifer, which in turn comes from Guinevere, who was of course King Arthur's wife. For a pretty, happy-go-lucky pet.

GINA – short for Georgina, with a touch of the dancehall floosie about it. If you've taken on an Italian Greyhound or Pointer, Gina could be quite becoming. Absolutely not for a pug-ugly.

Mainly for Cats

If It's a Him . . .

GABRIEL – although the archangel Gabriel was God's messenger, there is a hint of naughtiness about the name when applied to humans, and certainly when applied to cats. If you've got an extra-mischievous kitten, Gabriel will fit nicely. If he has a lot to say for himself, this will shorten to Gabby sooner, rather than later.

GARFIELD – after the famous cartoon pet (*see also Screen Stars*).

GERALD – German/Norman French, to do with kings and spears. For a master-mouser who's as likely to come through the cat-flap with a full-grown rabbit as with a tiny vole.

GODFREY – from old Anglo-Saxon for 'God's peace'. For the more thoughtful, rested kind of cat.

If It's a Her . . .

GENEVIEVE – she's got to be a real glamour-puss, because Genevieve is the patron saint of elegant Paris. But St Genevieve was also quite a fighter, in a good cause. For that rather special class of pet.

GEORGETTE – an elegant, expensive, don't-touch dress material, rather like those well-turned-out grey Persians.

GERTRUDE – from old German: it hasn't had much of a show in the UK since the thirties musical star Gertrude Lawrence and forties Gert and Daisy charlady double act, which could of course be what put paid to it. Cats notoriously hate being laughed at, so give this name to your pet only because you like it, not to be smart at her expense. She will not forgive.

GLADYS – such a joke name, you'd need to be extra-fond of her so that loads of affection made up for her social burden.

GLENDA – Welsh, we believe, for 'good girl'. In Britain, has acquired an unfortunate overtone from the fictitious columnist in *Private Eye* magazine, Glenda Slagg. Rescued to some extent by the fame of the real-life actress, now MP, Glenda Jackson.

GLORIA – Latin for 'glory'. Turned into a joke by the melodramacting of movie oldtimer Gloria Swanson and that splendidly, deliberately comic acting of Gloria Grahame. She has to be either a forbiddingly beautiful animal, or a bit of a comedy turn. (Don't worry, it's perfectly OK to laugh *with* a cat.)

GRACE – as in Grace and Favour, or the late Princess Grace Kelly of Monaco. A puss who tends not to steal from the dinner table under your very nose might be entitled to the name. So would a slinky blonde Burmese.

GRISELDA – from German for 'grey she-fighter'. Any questions?

Names for Dog *or* Cat

GAY/GAYE – Used to mean just that, and very nice, too. But these days . . .

GEMMA – Italian for 'jewel'. Since every pet dog or cat is a jewel in someone's eyes, it can suit all sorts.

GEORGINA – (*see GEORGE*). A Georgina can be much fluffier, more fripperish.

GERONIMO – Wild West fans might fancy this name, especially for any kind of attack dog or in-fighting alley cat.

GIGI – French heroine from a Colette novel that was turned into a hit musical movie. If a dog, she's got to be a real frou-frou: fully-decorated Toy Poodle, Maltese Terrier, Papillon, Small Continental Spaniel, Pekinese, Shih-tzu, Japanese Spaniel.

GILBERT – from German meaning, roughly, 'bright promise'. If a dog, perhaps a fun-loving one: Cairn or Norfolk Terrier, Beagle, Cocker Spaniel. A cat? Keep it for the triple-somersault specialist.

GILES – started life with an ancient Greek saint. With humans, for some reason, it is still the preserve of the toff. Accordingly, let us hand out Giles only to dogs as lordly as the Bloodhound, Great Dane, Tosa, Akita.

GISELLE – the dog has got to be utterly balletic, which takes us back to Afghan, Borzoi, Saluki. Also for an *exceptionally* pretty cat.

GORDON – Scots name, through and through. Dead cert for a Scottish Terrier.

GREGORY – from Greek for 'watchful'. So, let us examine our watchdogs: all the Collies, Old English Sheepdog, Samoyed, Tosa, Keeshond, Smooth Fox/Bull/Scottish/Tibetan Terriers. And the rest. For a cat, Gregory is dignified, weighty. Almost any cat could safely be called Gregory. If it appeals to you, we're sure he'll go along with it.

GUS/GUSSIE – short version of, and a bit of a comedown from, Augustus. For any playful Terrier or extra-impudent cat.

Mainly for Dogs

If It's a Him . . .

HADRIAN – after the Roman Emperor whose Wall still snakes across England's northern border, keeping the peevish Picts and surly Scots away from Wembley.

HAROLD – old North European name, meaning 'army and power', which didn't do King Harold of England a lot of good in 1066, when he tried to keep invader William off his patch, and got Conquered at Hastings, Sussex. Hard to think of a Dog Harold. Try it on a Dalmatian, Labrador or no-nonsense mid-sized mongrel who enjoys a good scrap but doesn't always expect to win.

HENRY – old German, should be reserved for the more serious type of dog. Have you ever seen a Bloodhound laugh?

HERBERT – apart from the derogatory 'He looks a right Herbert', this old German name has gone right out of fashion. We can't muster much enthusiasm for changing that, but there is bound to be a sturdy, independent dog who'll appreciate the importance of being Herbert.

HOMER – after the ancient Greek poet. One of the grand old names more popular in the United States than the UK. But it would suit a thoughtful-looking home-dog, such as a Labrador.

HORACE – after the ancient Roman poet, but remembering Horatio, the hero who held the bridge against incredible odds, more suited, perhaps, to an honest-to-goodness burglar-stopper.

HUGHIE – so different from the stolid Hugh that it springs from. For the real fun dog – pretty well any of the toy breeds.

If It's a Her . . .

HONEY – for small or smallish pet of the right colouring, from Chihuahua to Spaniel.

Mainly for Cats

If It's a Him . . .

HARRISON – just because we like the sound of it, really. Good one for fans of movie venturer Harrison Ford, of course.

HORATIO – (*see HORACE*).

If It's a Her . . .

HARRIET – offshoot of Henry/Henrietta. Strictly for a cottage cat.

HEATHER – pretty plant name for a quietly pretty puss.

HELOISE/ELOISE – tragic lover of scholar Pierre Abélard, in twelfth-century France. They wrote each other a lovely class of letter, but it all ended in tears. For that rarity, the utterly faithful cat.

HENRIETTA – female of Henry. Absolutely a fluffy-cat name.

HEPZIBAH – Hebrew, meaning 'delightful'.

HERMIONE – one of the old Greek mythical names, denoting a follower of the god Hermes. Two famous Hermiones in slightly more recent times: those supreme comediennes, the Misses Baddeley and Gingold. Dignified name for a prat-fall kind of puss.

HILDA – named after Princess in Northumberland, but more familiar through Hilda Ogden, who was a long-running star turn of TV's 'Coronation Street' soap serial. Hilda is Old English for 'battle', and our Hilda certainly spent her life head-butting the liberty-takers. So whether your new moggie is a prissy

Princess or a bit of a sharp-tongued Madam, she could be a Hilda.

HONORIA – it might be hard to tell while she's still a kitten, but for a name like this, she's going to have to be haughty. It means 'honour'. But it isn't going to stop her nicking your fresh-caught salmon off the kitchen sink.

HORTENSIA – another Latin one, to do with gardening. In the same league as Honoria. For the cat who looks a Little Flower, as opposed to Dustbin Raider.

HYACINTH – sweet name from a sweet-scented bloom, for a specially sweet little pet. (*See also JACINTA.*)

Names for Dog *or* Cat

HAMISH – Scottish version of James, but with a lip-smacking rascality to it.

HANNAH – stems from Ann (*see ANNIE*) for the honest working dog: Border Collie,

Beagle, Harrier, Bloodhound. Also the prissier ('Waiter, there's a fly on my roast turkey') kind of cat.

HARVEY – from the French Hervé, monk, wandering minstrel and saint. Might suit the dog or cat who gets around a lot and sings a good deal. We're not so sure about the sainthood. Keep in mind Harvey the Invisible Rabbit, if you have the kind of dog who insists on spending a lot of time in pubs.

HEBE – Greek goddess of youthfulness.

HEIDI – Austrian, made popular by a famous book and film of the same name. Is there an Austrian Hound on your farm? Very sweet name for a really pretty kitty.

HELGA – Scandinavian, meaning 'blessed'. As in: 'Now look what that blessed dog/cat has done!'

HERMAN – old folk will think instantly of Hitler's mate, Hermann Goering. For almost-as-old folk, it'll be the Herman's Hermits pop group. The name is German, meaning, roughly, 'soldier'. For a Doberman or German Shepherd, obvious but apt.

HESTER – from the same background as Esther, but with a slightly more severe sound to it. For the cat with the schoolma'am look.

HOLLY – after the attractive, prickly bush that brightens our Christmases. For a lively Chihuahua or spiky Siamese.

HUBERT – old German, meaning 'smart cookie'. There was a Saint Hubert in the eighth century. Hard to say how you'd tell if your pup is a likely Hubert. Just stand in front of the animal and see if the sound of it makes his tail wag, we suppose.

HUMPHREY – a name from Germany by way of Normandy. Extra-dignified, if slightly sad. For a Basset, naturally, or a Bulldog – or supremely imperious cat (*see VIPets*).

I

Mainly for Dogs

If It's a Him . . .

ISAAC – Biblical, the name given to a son born to Abraham, aged 100, and wife Sarah, aged ninety. Roughly translates as Here's a Fine Mess You've Got Me Into, Abie!

IVAN – (*see Saints and Sinners*).

If It's a Her . . .

IRMA – best-known from the old musical *Irma La Douce* (*Sweet Irma*). (*See EMMA*).

Mainly for Cats

If It's a Him . . .

IGNATIUS – from Latin for 'fiery'. This should suit the tiny mite who demands the Doberman's supper – and gets it.

ISADORE – an old Greek name associated with strength. If your pet can wrench open the oven, single-pawed, Isadore might suit.

IVOR – another one that the experts find hard to explain. A sturdy name, though: for a Bulldog or Pug, perhaps.

If It's a Her . . .

IDA – comes from Germany, but nobody really seems to know what, if anything, it means. Cockneys will certainly confuse it with Ada.

IMELDA – an Italian name, borne by a saint in the Middle Ages. Made more famous, more

60

recently, by the extravagances of Imelda Marcos of the Philippines. Perhaps for the dog who always goes for shoes? Elegant for a cat.

IMOGEN – from Scandinavia, where there was a god of peace called Ing. Consider it for that extra-mysterious one.

IRIS – flower name taken from goddess of Greek mythology who carried messages to the mortal world, travelling down a rainbow. Would suit a gorgeous Tortoiseshell Persian.

ISADORA – female of Isadore. Best-known holder of the name was Isadora Duncan, free-wheeling Greek dance star until 1927, when she carelessly trailed her scarf into the wheel of a moving car . . . Aaaaargh! Better warn the new kitten about those roads.

ISOBEL/ISABEL – a variation on Elizabeth. In Scotland, it developed pet versions including, suitably enough, Tibby. Perhaps best suited to a fairly severe madam of a moggie.

IVY – something to cling to, for the cat who absolutely has to sit on someone, or the dog whose nose is permanently at your heel.

J

Mainly for Dogs

If It's a Him . . .

JACK – historically derived from John. But would you ever call a gadabout Jack type John, as an alternative? Yes, admittedly we know a US Jack-the-Lad President famously flitted between the two, and indeed much else. Is Jack/Jackie too obvious for your J. Russell terrier? On the other hand, why not? Otherwise, consider Jack for any loyal, rather cheeky pet: Cairn, Yorkie, Dachshund.

JETHRO – another Biblical one, but you could really date yourself if you're thinking of the

Jethro Tull pop band. Or even the character from BBC Radio's 'Archers' soap serial. Better for a sturdy country dog: Setter, Pointer, Clumber, Dalmatian.

JOCK – for anything Scottish. He'll be proud to represent his nation.

JUSTIN – yet another of the old-time martyrs. Rather pretentious, we feel, for a pet. But if you think he can stand the snide yelpings of lesser breeds . . . a majestic St Bernard could cope.

If it's a Her . . .

JESSIE – fans of the notorious James bandit brothers will no doubt think over this one for the Pit Bull, Rottie, Dobie and so forth. In Scotland, we understand, it would not be a good idea to stand in a public place bellowing, 'Hey, Jessie!' in the vicinity of rough-looking fellows who don't know you.

JULIA – from Latin, of course, and just the ticket for a particularly imperious hound. Not necessarily big, though that always helps. Just above average in self-importance. For a Weimaraner or any of the Pointers, or tiny, proud Chihuahua.

Mainly for Cats

If It's a Him . . .

JAMES – a dignified name, borne by saints and kings, for the cat with a particular *hauteur*. The kind who will halt in mid-lick and stare you out for half an hour, if need be. And who, like any Royal personage, will never, ever be caught going to the toilet.

JARVIS – for some reason, although it comes from a martyr called Gervais, we feel this exudes a whiff of something sharp and shifty. Perhaps for the sassy puss who really ought to come on hoofing it in dickie-bow and spats.

JULIAN – as for Julia.

If It's a Her . . .

JACINTA – variation, believe or not, on Iris, and a good deal more elegant (no offence, Iris, luv).

JADE – beautiful name from the beautiful green gemstone. Not many jade-green cats in these parts, but plenty of sleek, jewel-like creatures who would suit such a name. It's also an obsolete expression for a worthless woman. With luck, not a lot of her catty friends will know that.

JANE/JANIE – female version of John (*see JACK*).

JASMINE – delightful flower name for a fragrant, fastidious pet.

JENNIFER – fresh, countrified name from creamy Cornwall, out of romantic King Arthur's Guinevere. If you ever find a totally honest cat (one that wouldn't take your kipper off the table, even if she'd heard the front door shut as you went out), Jennifer could be the name for her. If she turns out rather less of an angel, later on, *Jenny* doesn't need to be so utterly virtuous.

JESSICA – lovely, lyrical; nobody seems to know where it really comes from. Any lady cat ought to be proud to be a Jessica. So if you like the name, don't hesitate.

JOSEPHINA/JOSEFINA – classic feline name, versions of Josephine, made immortal by the wife of Emperor ('Not Tonight, Josephine') Napoleon.

Names for Dog *or* Cat

JAKE – raffish tag for a bit of a rascal. The kind of beast who is always vanishing over the wall or round the corner, a split second before your dustbin lid hits the tarmac. A Jake *dog* needs to be lean and a bit aggressive. A Jake *cat*, perhaps an extra touch of insolent independence.

JASON – from old Greek. It really means 'one

who heals', but we all think of Jason and his Argonauts, much more exciting chaps who boldly went where no Argonaut had gone before, and grabbed the Golden Fleece. Suits the more eager type of puppy – a Spaniel, certainly. With cats, perhaps a possible for the pet you don't quite see as a Jake.

JASPER – from Caspar, one of the Three Magi in the Bible. Unfortunately, we've all come to think of Dastardly Sir Jasper, Squire without a Heart, Having His Wicked Way. Could your cuddly little new ball of fur possibly grow into such a rascal? Better take a peek at the parents. Assuming he knows who they are . . .

JEMIMA – in the Bible, she was a daughter of that fount of woe, Job. But she wasn't born until Daddy had pulled through his endless troubles and got rich again. Which might explain why Jemima seems to us a slightly smug, smirky, never-known-a-day's-hunger type of name. Possibly more cat than dog, since cats are born to be smug. For a dog, an adult Shih-tzu (she needs the preposterous hairdo) or Japanese Spaniel.

JEREMIAH – he was the Biblical prophet who just never could find anything nice to forecast. Ideal for a truly mournful-looking Basset or Bloodhound. If he proves more cheerful than he looks, he can always become a jolly Jerry. Jeremiah would also fit the kind of cat who's bad news around the house, more often than not.

JONAH – he lived in a whale and had a terrible time. You get these pets who really don't mean any harm, but it happens to them anyway. Chair legs get chewed right through so that Grannie ends on her back in hospital; flower vases tip evil-smelling water on to your best carpet; someone samples His Master's Curry and then doesn't quite make it through the flap into the garden ... three major mishaps in the first twenty-four hours make him absolutely a Jonah.

JOSEPH – possibly better for cat than dog. For a dog, Joey or Joe sound much more fun.

K

Mainly for Dogs

If It's a Him . . .

KELVIN – Scottish origin, would clearly fit a Scottish/Border/Skye/Highland Terrier – or any other breed, in command of a suitably Scottish family.

KENNY – well, you wouldn't call him Kenneth, for Pete's sake, would you? (No offence to human Kenneths, but dogs are different.)

KERRY – as Irish as Irish can be, after the county. If you own a Kerry Blue Terrier, you might want to take the lazy way out and call her Kerry. It's an attractive name, anyway, and could suit lots of bright, beautiful dogs, Irish or not.

KIM – rather too much of a favourite for us to recommend to those seeking fresh, bright ideas for their pets. So we'll just remind you where it comes from and leave it to your own good judgement. Victorian author Rudyard Kipling, of course, made the name famous with his book, *Kim*. Nowadays it has mainly switched from male to female. Since we don't really recommend the name, we can hardly recommend it for any particular breed. But we bet there are more Alsatian Kims in this country than other dogs have had Bonios.

If It's a Her . . .

KELLY – from Ireland, of course, and, would you believe, connected with fighting? At a push, you can use it for a Him, as well.

KITTY – another version of Catherine. Perhaps not such a good idea for a tiny dog who might get mistaken for a cat. Too little a name for a really huge pet: but if yours is a playful, medium-size mongrel, Kitty would be just fine. And yes, it's OK for a cat as well. But if you're going to be that lazy, why did you spend money on this book?

Mainly for Cats

If It's a Him . . .

KARL – Teutonic version of Charles. Think of the too-clever-by-half Karl Marx.

KING – if a cat may look at a King, why shouldn't he *be* one, for Pete's sake?

KOMINSKY – why on earth, do we hear you inquire? Only because it was the real name of the great screen and stage comic Danny Kaye, whose decision to Omit the Ominsky helped him become a star. Is your cat funny enough to deserve it?

KURT – cut-down version of German Conrad. Sounds like one for a German Shepherd or Dachshund.

If It's a Her . . .

KARLA – (*see KARL*).

KATERINA – Continental variant of Catherine/
Katharine. The basic Greek name is generally
believed to have implied purity, but to us it
just demands a graceful romantic.

KIRI – as in Kiri te Kanawa, world-beating opera
star. For the cat who does a permanent purr-
along.

KOO – this familiar-sounding pet name might
be just right for a puss who is most at home
with the very best people.

Names for Dog *or* Cat

KATIE – still working the Catherine seam for all
it's worth. For the sweet little mongrel with
long curls, or the eager, friendly kitten.

KAY – same again, though a Kay can perhaps
be a bit more independent than a Katie.

KYLIE – soap-star singer whose name entirely escapes us put this one on the world map. Go on – but don't hit people if they laugh!

L

Mainly for Dogs

If it's a Him . . .

LARRY – a touch of nostalgia for anybody who remembers Larry the Lamb of old-time radio's Toytown. Alternatively, it comes (rather a long way round) from old Gaelic Lorcan, meaning 'small fierce person'. Sounds like a Shih-tzu, Brussels Griffon or most of the little terriers.

LENNY/LENNIE – strictly for a fun dog, the kind you're likely to bring home from Battersea. No breeding, but a bundle of entertainment.

LESTER – if you've been a fan of champion jockey Lester Piggott, think of this one for your Greyhound or Whippet.

LEX – short form of Alexander, but the kind of name to confuse a passing Japanese.

If It's a Her . . .

LARA – remember the heroine Lara's theme, from the *Dr Zhivago* movie? Elegant name for an elegant tragedienne such as the sad-visaged Shar-pei, the wrinkly Chinese Fighting Dog. If you feel sadder than her when you take away your slipper, she's a Lara.

Mainly for Cats

If it's a Him . . .

LOUIS/LOUIE/LOU – in its full dignity, Louis is the name of Kings (of France, naturally). Louie or Lou would be affectionate enough for less exalted, perhaps one-eared, cross-eyed pets.

LUDOVIC – stems from Louis, but has a princely Middle European tinge to it.

If It's a Her . . .

LAURA – Latin for 'Laurel' (which also makes an attractive and out-of-the-ordinary name).

LAVINIA – from one of ancient Rome's mythical tales: she was a King's daughter and wife of the first Roman, Aeneas. Snooty name for a snooty-puss.

LETITIA – Latin word for 'joy', shortens, of course, to Letty (if you must). It also shortens to Lettice, but who needs jokes about whether *Lettuce* likes *salad*?

LIBBY – pet-name version of Elizabeth.

LOUELLA – from Lou(ise) + Ella. OK if your pet looks a bit of a Southern Belle or perhaps Country and Western.

LUCASTA – made-for-the-sale name by poet Richard Lovelace, 300 years ago ('To Lucasta,

Going to the Wars'). If you like the sound of it, why not?

LYDIA – really elegant, but also irresistibly reminds us of the old music hall song, 'Lydia the Tattooed Lady'. So you could say it suits a real patchwork puss.

Names for Dog *or* Cat

LANA – female version of ancient Celtic Alan. Made famous by old-time movie glamourette Lana Turner. For the slinky, I-need-luxury-comforting pet.

LEO – meaning, of course, 'lion'. A dog? Yorkshire or Staffordshire Bull Terrier, among others.

LEROY – from French *'le roi'* – 'the King'. For the tower-block Alsatian. A cat? Well, every cat's a monarch, in his own estimation.

LINUS – made a household name by Linus of

the *Peanuts* cartoon strip, who desperately clung to his comfort blanket.

LISA – (*see ELIZABETH*).

LUCY – cosy fireside name for a cosy fireside pet. For something slightly different and much, much grander, try Lucia.

LULU – strictly for the pretty, flirtatious dog (Toy Poodle, Cairn) or a real floosie of a cat.

M

Mainly for Dogs

If It's a Him . . .

MACK – if your pet has pearly teeth, dear, like the shark in the old song, 'Mack the Knife'. . .

MANNY – from the immensely dignified Emmanuel, but the shortened form has a strong whiff of highly undignified, rascally fun. You wouldn't call your giant Akita Manny unless he had naughtily killed, cooked and eaten someone you didn't much like. But for a roguish Dachshund, or the cat who always smells slightly of stolen sardines, absolutely right.

If It's a Her . . .

MADONNA – problem with this name, nowadays, is you'd never know where she'd been.

MAGGIE – yet another Margaret extraction. Suits a confident, not too ladylike, mongrel.

MARINA – one of the British Royal family names; it's also what they call a yacht basin with petrol pump and sandwich bar. This could be the only name for your new pet, but to us, it seems a little flavourless. Just ask yourself what you'll say when people inquire: 'Why Marina?'

MARISA – attractive, rather posh Spanish variant of Mary. If you happen to have a Spanish Greyhound or Mastiff around the house, she'll love it.

Mainly for Cats

If It's a Him . . .

MILES/MILO – on the whole, when we hear of a Miles, we think, unfairly, of a cad. And as for Milo! Miles offers the superficial dignity of a slightly tipsy con man with his credit cards in the other suit. Milo is his rascally continental counterpart, with an eye for the ladies, a half-offer of marriage and a plane to catch. If your pet seems lovable but cunning . . .

If It's a Her . . .

MABEL – nice old-fashioned name for a nice old-fashioned tabby who'd look right in a housemaid's outfit if she was 100 per cent human.

MADGE – from Margaret. Like Mabel, old-fashioned – but perhaps more flighty, we feel.

MARIGOLD – for a cat who's anything like the colour of the flower. If you like this pretty name enough, of course, then to heck with her colour!

MATILDA – old German, to do with fighting and fighters, though a Matilda cat would sound far too prim and schoolma'amish to get herself involved in *that* type of carry-on.

MILDRED – from the Anglo-Saxon for 'strong and gentle'. Cut out for a fairly prim, reserved type of puss.

MILLICENT – from the French Melisande, which might take your fancy instead. It shortens, sweetly enough, to Millie.

MINERVA – the original was an ancient Roman goddess. Pretentious, perhaps? Don't worry: just announce it with all the confidence at your command and a large bowl of tasty fish at the ready. She'll learn to love it. Honestly.

MIRANDA – said to have been invented by Shakespeare for his heroine in *The Tempest*. Curiously under-used, for such an attractive name. For the moggie with added mystery.

Names for Dog *or* Cat

MAGNUS – Latin for 'great'. So if you're trying to name a Great Dane, Bloodhound, Rottweiler, St Bernard, look no further. With a cat (don't ask us why) we don't feel he needs to be all that big to become a Magnus – except, perhaps, in personality.

MAMIE – one of the dozens of variations of Mary. This one, unlike solid dependable Mary, is a flibbertygibbet name: ideal for an extrovert dog or fancy-free cat.

MANDY – short for Amanda.

MARLON – if he's overweight, walks with a scowl and a swagger and has this quite compelling presence . . .

MARTY – from Martin, which was in turn out of Mars, the noted Roman god and choc bar. You probably wouldn't call an animal Martin, because it just doesn't seem one of those names. But try Marty for a cheeky little rogue of a pet.

MAUDIE – a version of Matilda. Cheeky name for a saucebox Dachsie or mischievous kitten.

MAX/MAXIE – after the original, long-gone, Cheeky Chappie comic, Max Miller.

Obviously for the perky, impudent Yorkie or Dachshund, or for the puss who does tricks.

MAXIMILIAN – the full-rig version of Max. If he's a dog, this is strictly For Emperor Material Only. He has got to be either majestic King-size or a very small, very special, very self-assured little Princeling. Maximilian just will not do, we feel, for any in-between kind of dog. A lesser breed is never going to grow into this one. If he's a cat, he can get away with being nondescript in size: but he still needs to be the commanding sort of person you give up your seat to (after dusting it, carefully).

MEG – a really gipsyish name for the pet who's a compulsive roamer (a quirk you may not yet have had time to find out about). Also suggests mystic soothsaying qualities – the kind of dog or cat who senses whether you have *quite* shut the fridge door.

MISCHA – Russian diminutive of Michael. For Him, it has the tilted-titfer touch of an émigré nobleman. For Her, it conveys the perfumed allure of a lady who will bestow her cosmopolitan favours, not cheaply, but most enthusiastically.

MONTY – to the World War Two generation, this would at once bring to mind the autocratic hero of the Battle of Alamein, Field-Marshal Bernard M. To people of the seventies, the absurd TV antics of 'Monty Python's Flying Circus'. Hero or clown: take a look at him and guess. Monty is also short for Montague, which would suit a battered-topper, seedy-spats, spare-us-a-kipper-Guv kind of cat.

MYRTLE – beautifully old-fashioned name of a plant that used to be favourite for bridal bouquets.

N

Mainly for Dogs

If It's a Him . . .

NAT – nippy name for a zippy little dog: Jack Russell, Whippet. Short for Nathaniel (*see Cats*).

NATHAN – was an Old Testament prophet, social-affairs adviser to King David and King Solomon (who'd have thought *he* needed advice!) For the dog who's a bit cleverer than average.

NICK – if he's a bit of a mischievous little devil, name him after Old Nick himself. Short, of course, for Nicholas, which seems to us more cat than dog.

If It's a Her ...

NELLIE – comes from both Helen and Eleanor, neither of which is really a doggy name. But if the lady's a bit of a scamp, she'll make a Nellie.

Mainly for Cats

If It's a Him ...

NAHUM – resounding name from the Old Testament. He was, of course, a prophet.

NATHANIEL – originally Hebrew: he was an Apostle.

NORMAN – less boring on a cat, we feel, than on a human. Try it, anyway: the worst he can do is ignore you.

If It's a Her . . .

NANCY – for the oldsters who still remember the Sinatra song, this could do for the Cat with the Laughing Face.

NANETTE – from Ann (*see ANNA/ANNIE, HANNAH*). If there's such a thing as an extra-dainty cat, Nanette should suit her.

NAOMI – another Bible name, meaning 'pleasant'. If you like it, try it, in these early days when she's still more concerned with what there is to eat than what you call her.

NATALIA/NATALIE – by a tortuous linguistic route which we won't go into, it's originally from Noel, the day Jesus Christ was born. For the slim and slinky model, we feel, rather than the fireside Podge.

NERISSA – from old Greek mythology and the daughters of sea god Nereus. As with Natalia, for the elegant feline, rather than the plump and ploddy.

NICOLA – feminine version of Nicholas.

Names for Dog *or* Cat

NADIA – from the Russian for 'hope'. For a slinky Saluki, agile Afghan or balletic Borzoi, of course, but would not sound amiss for a lithe Dalmatian.

NICHOLAS – from old Greek: there was a St Nicholas in the Middle East, in the fourth century A.D. The name is more renowned in its corrupted form, Santa Claus. Good crisp name for a businesslike cat.

NINA – Russian variation of Ann/Anna. Suits a big Pointer or Wolfhound – or little Papillon, Brussels Griffon, Maltese Terrier, as long as you don't lapse into calling her Ninny.

NINOTCHKA – even more exotically Russian than Nina.

O

Mainly for Dogs

If It's a Him . . .

ODDBOD – lots of us have come home with a pup whose ancestry is shrouded in the thickest of mist. Keep Oddbod in mind for that joyous occasion.

ODDJOB – after James Bond movie character, of course.

OLIVER – not many of us remember Cromwell personally, but Oliver is distinguished enough for your canine Lord Protector (Mastiff, Rottweiler, Samoyed, Staffordshire or

Tibetan Terrier, miniature Schnauzer . . . any of the first-class watchdogs, whatever their size). Oliver also suits the pet who isn't afraid to ask for more. Ollie, the short form, is jolly enough for any pet.

If It's a Her . . .

OLYMPIA – traditional home of the Greek gods. She'll have to be utterly superior in every way.

Mainly for Cats

If It's a Him . . .

ORLANDO – the original Marmalade Cat. He needs to be big, fat and cuddly, with a purr like a BMW racing bike. And, of course, orange-coloured: absolutely none other will do.

OSBERT – favoured by the upper lisping classes of the last century and was of course the name of one of the smirking Sitwells. If your cat seems too clever for his own good, think over Osbert. (If he turns out to be a real Osbert, by the way, never *ever* cut him down to Ossie, let alone Oz. He will have you barred from all the best addresses in town.)

OSRIC – treat as for Osbert.

If It's a Her . . .

OCTAVIA – superb name, from ancient noble Rome, for the really haughty pet who can hardly bring herself to accept your humble hospitality.

OTIS – from Otto (*which also see*). Rarefied, made famous by Cole Porter with 'Miss Otis Regrets', Miss Otis, you may remember the manservant telling us, woke up and found her dream of love was gone, so got a gun and shot her lover down. For the rich, romantic and ruthless feline.

Names for Dog *or* Cat

OBERON – since he was King of the Fairies, you may like to pause and consider before giving this otherwise splendid name to, say, a sweet little beribboned Toy Poodle. A Bulldog or Mastiff, on the other hand, could get away with it for you. Also right for a particular fey kind of cat.

ODETTE – French, of course, from an original German word meaning 'rich'. Which could help you with a name for that soon-to-be-pampered toy-almost-anything. With a cat, this one should be reserved for the luxury-loving coquette (which hardly restricts the field all that much!)

OLGA – if you've got an Olga-the-Beautiful-Spy creature, such as the Borzoi, Saluki or Afghan, the choice is made for you. A cat can be a lot cuddlier to look at, and still be an Olga.

OPHELIA – if you have the kind of nerve and neighbours to be able to bellow this beautiful Shakespearean name from the doorstep, you could hardly find one more suited to a Collie, Setter ... or even a Doberman. Not really for little stumpy dogs, though a gorgeous long-haired Dachshund could probably take it, by sheer sex appeal. If a cat, preferably a long-haired breed, such as Persian.

ORPHEUS – in myth, a Greek musician so amazing that after his wife, Eurydice, died, he was able to play his way into Hell, pick her up and carry her back to life – on condition he did not once look back. In these stories, of course, they always do the wrong thing. So Eurydice ended up pouring the Retsina at her place, instead of his. Glum kind of tale, but a good strong name for bellowing at a dog or murmuring to a silky cat. Just as long as they're not at all musical . . .

OSCAR – went out of favour a little after people heard about the scandalous goings-on of Oscar Wilde. But we're not quite so choosy these days, and anyway, the Hollywood Academy Awards have put Oscar back on a pedestal. For any dog or cat you think is a pet to be prized, award him the Oscar.

OTTO – from German for 'rich' and 'prosperous'.

It's a nicely rakish, Mittel-European name to give to your Bosnian Hound, Weimaraner, Pomeranian, or (if Dracula fails to appeal), your Transylvanian Hound.

P

Mainly for Dogs

If It's a Him . . .

PETE/PETEY – for the dog who may not look much at the start, but tends to grow on you. Why not Peter, in full? Just doesn't sound right, to us, on a dog, that's all . . .

PHIL – same as for Pete.

PIERCE – good, swashbuckling name for an imposing dog, especially Great Dane or Mastiff. It's linked to Peter, by the way.

If It's a Her . . .

PEG/PEGGY – another of the names that spring from Margaret. 'Peg o' My Heart' . . . 'Sweet Peggy O'Neil' . . . it certainly packs plenty of affection.

PENNY – (*see PENELOPE*).

Mainly for Cats

If It's a Him . . .

PEREGRINE – another of those aristo names. Sometimes favoured by the lower middle classes to give their boy a boot up the social scale. No reason why you shouldn't do the same for your cat.

If It's a Her . . .

PANSY – from the pretty flower, of course. Think of Pansy for a really petite puss.

PENELOPE – in Greek myth, the supremely faithful wife of Odysseus, who spent a lot of time away from the family and eventually turned up with some tale about having been on a bit of an Odyssey. Penelope is for the cat who is yours alone, even when you've forgotten to pay the milkman. Not really for a dog, though Penny would be fine.

PERSEPHONE – one of a long line of Greek goddesses. Tell her it's pronounced Per-sef-uh-nee, by the way.

PHILOMENA – in Ireland she used to be thought a saint, but turned out to be only a wrongly-read inscription in a tomb. Which leaves us with just a very pretty name, and what's so bad about that?

PRISCILLA – from the Bible: she was one of the first Christian activists. How that information is supposed to help you judge whether it would suit your cat, Heaven knows. Shortens to Cilla, of course.

PRUDENCE – from old Latin roots, it means what it says. A question of whether the name appeals to you, really. We just thought you'd like to know it was available.

PRUNELLA – another from the Latin, this time Roman 'Gardener's World': *prunus*, or 'plum tree'. If you are a fan of that excellent British actress Prunella (H.M. the Queen) Scales, you might go for this.

Names for Dog *or* Cat

PANDORA – best known for the ancient Greek myth about the woman who couldn't keep her hands off the secret box that, unfortunately, held all the troubles of mankind. There are dogs and cats like that. If you're landed with a specially mischievous one, at least Pandora is a stately, gracious name.

PEGASUS – he was the fabulous flying horse in another of the Greek legends. For a fantastically fleet-footed Greyhound or Whippet – or a cat who can outrun the local bullyboy Tom.

PERCY – aristo name of olde, olde Uppe-Northe

English family, originally French. Given a touch of pointed vulgarity, alas, by our Australian offshoots, but a traditional Percy does not deign to be aware of such low matters.

PERDITA – not necessarily something you'd want to call your dog *or* cat, since it basically means 'lost'. It would depend on her habits, we suppose. Anyway, it's a good name for a slightly wanton woman. If a dog, it should suit most of the toy breeds. If a cat, one who can seduce you into getting the tin-opener out even before you've got the kettle on for yourself.

PHOEBE – you wouldn't necessarily think of this for your American Pit Bull, but otherwise it's OK for any size or make of dog, from Great Swiss Mountain to Mexican Hairless.

PIA – comes from Italy, sister version of Pius. Weigh up whether you could cope with being asked, continually: 'Does she Pia lot, then?'

POLLY – no reason why the parrot world should be allowed sole rights to Polly. Just as good for a joyous, no-special-breed dog-about-the-house, or an easygoing sort of cat.

POPPY – from the beautiful bright red bloom. Treat as for Polly.

Q/R

Mainly for Dogs

If It's a Him ...

RAB – Scots short form of Robert, from the German for 'shining fame'. We don't quite see Robert itself as a pet name, though you may well disagree. Rab (or Rabbie), on the other hand, would certainly seem to suit any of the tartan-clad Scottish Terriers.

RED – short for Redmond, an Irish favourite. So you could pick it for your flame-haired Irish

Setter, or your huge but not-so-flaming Irish Wolfhound.

RICK – usually short for Richard. Made particularly well-known by that terribly brave and gritty American chap in that bar in the movie *Casawotsit*, played by Humphrey Thingammyjig. Got to be a lip-curling Alsatian or similar, hasn't he – though a Shih-tzu curls a pretty mean lip, too.

ROD – short for Roderick, a German-rooted name, or Rodney. Come to think of it, if he's a fine upstanding animal, what's wrong with Roderick, anyway? Somehow, we can't bring ourselves to recommend Rodney. Most unfair, but . . .

ROGER – they can go on as long as they like about the complicated European antecedents of Roger. To most true-born Brits, he will be Roger the Lodger, for reasons better not explicitly explained. One thing you can be sure of: Roger is all bounce and no pedigree.

ROLF – from Ralph, has to do with wolves. We hardly need to point out which breeds, given that explanation, might suit Rolf.

RUFUS – from Latin meaning 'redhead'. Another one for the Ginger Tendency.

If It's a Her . . .

QUEENIE – a comfortably settled name for a back-street pub dog of no fixed breed, or a retirement-home cat.

ROXY – because we feel you would not, on the whole, want to go the whole hog and call your pet an over-the-top Roxana. Was there ever a real Roxana? Indeed there was . . . She was an Asian Princess who married Alexander the Great and more or less had to because he whacked the living daylights out of her dad's army around 300 years B.C. and had a son who became Alexander the Fourth who helped to rule his father's empire, only he and his mum got themselves murdered . . . Are you sure your new pet is up to all this?

Mainly for Cats

If It's a Him . . .

QUENTIN – from Latin *quintus*, meaning 'fifth'. If he's the fifth member of your family – or even pet number five – this would be subtly suitable. So of course, would Quintus.

RAFAEL – variant of Raphael (nothing really wrong with that version, if you prefer it). Raphael the Healer was one of the archangels or superangels, alongside Gabriel and Michael. We doubt that you'd find true Archangel qualities in any cat. A longhair Persian would probably consider himself a rung or two above archangel status, but if it's a question of Whiskas or no Whiskas . . .

If It's a Her . . .

RACHEL – name of a Biblical beauty. A really lovely name for a cat who doesn't actually need to be *that* beautiful, by the generous standards of us cat-lovers.

RAQUEL – there's really only been the one, hasn't there? Your puss will have to be especially statuesque to warrant being granted Miss Welch's starry name. An Abyssinian could probably cope.

Names for Dog *or* Cat

QUINCY – also from *quintus*, lately better-known for American TV series which starred Jack Klugman. Well, at least it's fairly unusual. Another for either dog or cat.

REBECCA – Biblical, possibly (we're told) meaning 'cow'. But you can just forget we said that, and it really is a beautiful name. Be warned that the Bible Rebecca (or Rebekah) was a thoroughly bossy person who couldn't tolerate being thwarted.

REGINA – Latin for 'queen', as we all know. A royalist dog-lover could take it seriously, especially for a Buck House-pattern Corgi or Dorgi (Corgi-cum-Dachshund). On the whole, though, it sits better on a queenly cat than a doggy dwarf act.

REUBEN – in the Bible he was Jacob's oldest lad. It has a bit of a roll to it, but would probably soon come down to Rube.

REX – given the swarming horde of Rex dogs on this planet, we'd suggest this for your cat. Or for a long, long rest (*see Top Ten Names for Pets*). Society note: a Rex is usually married to a Regina (*which also see*) and they both wear crowns. On the whole, though, we'd help found the Society Against Calling Any More Dogs Rex This Century.

RHODA – from the Greek for 'rose'. You could always help promote it back into popularity, if you're keen.

RHYS – old Welsh warrior name. Obviously right for a brave Welsh Terrier.

RITA – from Margaret by way of Margarita. It seems to have been mainly a showbiz choice, from the super-glam Rita Haywoth to the terribly homegrown Rita Tushingham and the 'Coronation Street' soap serial's character Rita Fairclough/Sullivan (as was). Probably for the dog (no offence, ladies) who's extra-entertaining, or the cat you otherwise couldn't have thought of a name for.

RORY – mainly Irish, meaning 'redhead'. Irish Setter, naturally, but no reason why any spirited dog shouldn't carry the name. Tell him to go for it! A cat? Well, he's preferably a ginger tom, isn't he?

ROSE/ROSIE – make it Rose *or* Rosie for your cat, just Rosie for a dog. Why? Trust our intuition - you've paid for it! Loads of variations on offer, by the way: Rosa, Rosalie, Roseanna, to name but a couple. For a Rose or a Rosie (or any of the variations) we feel breed simply doesn't matter: it's a name for a lovable pet, and that is *that*!

RUBY – nice, barmaidy name from turn of the century. Shame it hasn't stayed with us, much. Another of those names for the cosiest of one-person dogs or fireside cats.

RUPERT – was there ever such a famous bear, apart from Winnie the Pooh? Perhaps more pooch than puss, but you'll know a Rupert as soon as you see him.

S

Mainly for Dogs

If It's a Him . . .

SAM – cut-down Samuel (*see Cats*). For the
friendly, obliging dog who's no show-off.
Sammy, too, of course.

SCOTTY/SCOTTIE – over-obvious for any of
the Scottish breeds, but 'Star Trek' fans might
fancy naming a pet after Beam Me Up, Scotty.
Not for any of the big, noble breeds.

SHANE – became popular after the Alan Ladd
Western of the fifties. Probably best for

German Shepherd, Doberman, or any mixture
with sharp nose and teeth.

If It's a Her . . .

SADIE – a real barmaid of a name, though you
don't hear it much, these days. It's a shortening of Sarah, which means Princess in
Hebrew. But if Sadie *was* a Princess, she'd be
the one getting the Royal family name in the
papers, for all the wrong reasons! Remember
naughty Miss Sadie Thompson in Somerset
Maugham's story, 'Rain'? Keep this for the
really roguish dog who just wants to lavish
her love on everyone.

SHEENA – one of a whole splatter of names
that starts with Jane.

Mainly for Cats

If It's a Him . . .

SAMUEL – another name from old Israel. Once
you get used to each other, this will no doubt
come down to Sammy or Sam (*see Dogs*).

SEPTIMUS – Nice schoolroom-sounding name for the cat for whom *seven* has some special meaning in his life. The seventh kitten in a litter, perhaps. Or, if you're really cat-crazy, the seventh puss in your family.

SEYMOUR – sounds a bit of a know-all: if you get a Seymour, watch that well-laid table when he's around.

SIDNEY/SYDNEY – from the French Saint-Denis, probably better saved for a fairly comical moggie. It's a feminine as well as masculine name, but to avoid confusion all round, we'd advise keeping it as a boy's name.

SOLOMON – famous old King of Bible times, who showed his great wisdom, faced with a claim by two mothers to the same baby, by suggesting they cut it up and take half each (just his little way of working out which woman *really* loved the child like a mother).

SYLVESTER – well, the old song, 'I Tawt I Taw a Puddy Tat' (translation: 'I Thought I Saw a

Pussy Cat'), sung by a nervous cage-bird, indicates the kind of Puddy Tat to carry this name. Crafty is as crafty does, we say . . .

If It's a Her . . .

SAMANTHA – made famous around the world by the character (and song) in the movie *High Society*, and in Britain, at least, by a well-formed girl called Samantha Fox. It certainly suits a plush long-haired Persian.

SAPPHIRE – a jewel name for a quality cat. Something like a Turkish Angora, for example.

SARAH – the respectable Princess who tries to hide sister Sadie from the public gaze. Strictly for the puss who keeps herself clean about the ears.

Names for Dog *or* Cat

SABRINA – sounds very Latin, but goes back to British mythology: the River Severn in

Gloucestershire is named after a Sabrina who was chucked in it and drowned on orders from her wicked stepmother. If we draw a polite veil over the drowning part of the story, this is a lovely name for a Setter or Great Spitz, or a beautiful Sealpoint Balinese cat.

SACHA – a touch of old Mother Russia in this pet form of (believe it or not) Alexander. Over there, it's a male name; over here, we may think of Sacha more as feminine. A male Sacha, we feel, should be a swaggering smoothie: female, a slinky seductress. And that goes for both dogs and cats.

SALLY – another name extracted from Sarah, but unlike Sadie, Sally will be a respectable, settled-by-the-fireside kind of creature. Any lady Labrador could be a Sally. So could any plump little tabby cat.

SELINA – probably after Greek goddess of the moon, Selene. Reserved, we feel, for a specially silky dog – well-groomed Yorkie or Irish Setter – or luxury-class cat, such as a Red Peke-face Persian.

SERENA – from the Latin for (surprise!) 'serene'. Pleasant name for a cat who doesn't go looking for trouble.

SIEGFRIED – now *here's* a name and a half! It's German, of course, best known from nineteenth-century composer Richard Wagner's opera set, *Ring of the Nibelung*. A great romantic, our Siegfried, if that's any clue . . .

SIMON/SIMEON – was one of the biblical Apostles. For a lady, Simone is an attractive variant.

STANLEY – either puts you in mind of the great old English aristo family which produces the Earls of Derby, or Stan of Laurel and Hardy (not to mention the great Stanley Holloway). We don't feel your pet can quite sustain the nobler side of Stanley: it's not that kind of name. If he's a bit of a comedian, though . . .

STELLA – not too many human Stellas around, these days. It's from Latin for 'star'. Probably better for a big, imposing dog or sweet little cat.

SUSAN – from Susanna, meaning 'lily'. Ideal for a real cottage kitty. If she's a little on the flighty side, try the French variation, Suzette – or, even more coquettish, Sukie.

T

Mainly for Dogs

If it's a Him . . .

TAM – Scottish for Tom. Another likely bet for your Scottish/Skye/West Highland Terrier.

TERRY – for pretty well any type of Terrier, unless you think that's being too obvious. Fine for the happy-yappy puppy who's a mongrel and proud of it.

THOR – the Norsemen's war god. As long as you're not the sort of dumb animal who indulges in dog-fights, you couldn't find a stronger name for a big, strong dog . . . or a wee small cushion-size canine who feels every bit as mighty as a Tosa, but just hasn't learned about size.

TIM – short for Timothy which we feel is better on a cat (*see Cats*). Probably the bright, alert kind of dog who does what he's asked, more or less.

TYRONE – after the county in Ireland, made forever famous by American movie swashbuckler Tyrone Power. We think it sounds as Power-packed as some of his all-action films, so think of Tyrone for a muscular mutt.

If It's a Her . . .

TRIXIE – a pet version of Beatrice. Neat little name for nice-natured friend.

TRUDIE – another pet version, this time from Gertrude.

Mainly for Cats

If It's a Him . . .

TANTALUS – in those old Greek tales of gods, monsters and amazing deeds, Tantalus was King of Lydia, but that didn't save him being condemned to eternal hunger and thirst. You may well find you have taken on someone like that . . .

TEDDY – for one of those chubby-cheek, tubby-tum moggies who could double as a singing hotwater bottle.

TIMOTHY – from the Greek for 'god worshipper'. Timothy was right-hand man to Paul the Apostle. It shortens, obviously, to Tim or Timmy, which we feel is a waste of a dignified name.

If It's a Her . . .

TABITHA – from a Middle Eastern word for 'gazelle', shortening, of course, to Tabby. And you can't get a pussier name than that.

Reverse the process: first catch your tabby, then call her Tabitha. In full, please. At all times!

THEODORA/THEODORE – Greek for 'god's gift'. If you think your pet is just that, and he/she thinks the same, what are we waiting for? One of the few names that loses no dignity when shortened – to Theo/Thea.

TIFFANY – remember the movie, *Breakfast at Tiffany's*? If your pet has the delicious looks of a young Audrey Hepburn, what better name than this? It has verve, it has style.

Names for Dog *or* Cat

TAMARA – old Russian, needs a fairly posh pet to carry it off. Afghan/Saluki, again? Equally right for a cat who can look at a Queen and not be stared out.

TAMSIN – a feminine variant of Thomas/Thomasina, from Cornwall. It has an alert sort of ring to it. For the dog who cocks his ears at you a lot, or the cat who tends to sit up like an unblinking statue.

TARA – from Ireland (where it's a renowned and ancient patch of County Meath) by way of *Gone with the Wind*, in which Vivien Leigh scooped up frantic handfuls of her Suth'un estate and vowed never to live in a cardboard box again. Your pet doesn't have to be Irish to be a Tara, but it helps if she's fairly dramatic.

TARQUIN – the last King of ancient Rome was a Tarquin. He also was the sort who gave kingship a bad name by murdering people. It was all his fault that Rome went republican. But he was a long time ago and it's a great name for a great big handsome dog – perhaps a Great Dane, Mastiff or Weimaraner. For a cat, size doesn't seem to us to matter quite so much, as long as he's extra-proud.

THEA/THEO – from Theodora/Theodore (*which see*).

THEOBALD – old German meaning, approximately, 'brave lad'. Plenty of dogs it would be ideal for: a battling little Terrier or perhaps a big Rottweiler. Sounds quite good on a handsome Boxer, too. With a new kitten, it's pretty hard to tell how rough 'n' tough he'll turn out to be. But if he loves to leap at your knees and hang on by his claws 'n' teeth, he could grow into a Theobald.

THOMAS – honest, no-nonsense name made famous by a doubting saint and a busy-busy tank engine. For the kind of straight-dealing dog who goes straight to his bowl at feeding time, straight to the door at walkies time, and straight for the burglar at break-in time.

TITUS – from old Rome, which had a mighty Emperor Titus. Some people went off the name a bit 300 years ago when Titus Oates was unmasked as an anti-papist plotter. But it's a resounding name for a powerful Mastiff, Newfoundland, Rottweiler or Great Dane – or for a small but fearless Shih-tzu or Toy Terrier. A king-size cat can certainly bear this name with pride, too.

TOBIAS – from Greek for 'god is good', was a

character in Bible times who went around with a dog and an archangel (Raphael). Later, a dog called Tobias, a.k.a. Toby, became Mr Punch's pet in the now-defunct humour magazine. For a droll dog or comedy cat.

U

Mainly for Dogs

If It's a Him ...

ULICK – an Irish name, probably out of Hugh: near irresistible for a dog who's an obsessive hygienist.

Mainly for Cats

If It's a Him ...

URIAH – Biblical King who got himself killed, though not for tearing up the new potted plants. Given an unfortunate, probably non-erasable odour of the office creep by Charles

Dickens's hand-wringing, drip-nosed character, Uriah Heep. There are highly lovable cats, of course, who put on a fair imitation of Heep . . . try it.

Names for Dog *or* Cat

ULRIC/ULRICA – after assorted saints, English and German. In Olde Englishe it means something like 'powerful wolf'. Your German Shepherd, obviously, could be a satisfactory Ulric/Ulrica. Among cats, since Ulrica sounds as though she ought to be a beautiful Princess with long, luxuriant tresses, a gorgeous Longhair Persian would carry the name with tremendous style. A feline Ulric, on the other hand, ought to be a stubby, nightclub-bouncer kind of cat.

V

Mainly for Dogs

If It's a Him . . .

VICTOR – male version of Victoria (*which see*), meaning 'victory' in Latin.

If It's a Her . . .

VIRGINIA – from the State of Virginia, USA, named after the Virgin Queen Bess. It shortens to Ginny, but perhaps you could prevent that, for the sake of a most attractive name.

Mainly for Cats

If It's a Him . . .

VERNON – if he's been lucky enough to be rescued through an animal shelter, you could name him after the football pool.

If It's a Her . . .

VANESSA – sounds as if it ought to be right for a *Country Life* class of dog: on the other hand, in a crowd of county folk, she might get confused with a hundred and one human Vanessas, all within earshot. Want to take the chance? OK: we think Vanessa would suit any big, sleek sporting dog. And if you have got yourself a really vain cat who's always preening herself, she's almost certainly a Vanessa, too.

VENETIA – wow, what a superior name, to be sure! It's Latin for that most lovely of cities, Venice. Save it for the most beautiful of cats.

VIOLET – lovely flower name for a gentle, rather shy little puss.

Names for Dog *or* Cat

VERONICA – originally a saint. Pleasing name for an athletic country pet, perhaps: Pointer, Setter, Dalmatian, Cocker/Springer Spaniel. Also for the slinkier type of cat.

VICTORIA – richly elegant name: all gold goblets and purple velvet. For a regally beautiful Irish Setter, Greyhound, Afghan, a queenly Chow Chow – or Little-Princess-size Lhasa Apso. Or the Queen Victoria lookalike Japanese Spaniel.

VIRGIL – after the grand old Latin poet. Frankly, we are not sure what kind of dog or cat to suggest as a potential Virgil. Just as long as he *looks* poetic . . .

W

Mainly for Dogs

If It's a Him . . .

WALDO – old German indicating a 'man of power'. Right for a mighty Mastiff, or for a teeny Peke who gets his own way just as surely, by yapping long enough.

WARREN – female fans of movie star Beatty might consider this one. Especially if your pet is, um, over-active in matters of romance.

WAYNE – for the dog who wishes he was a bit more like the characters John Wayne played, in rather too many movies. We'd put it in our canal-towpath, piece-of-string, motor-bike-in-kitchen bracket, frankly. But if you like it, why not?

If It's a Her . . .

WANDA – old Polish name made particularly famous by that film, *A Fish Called Wanda*. If you're trying to name a dog, rather than a guppy, it could suit a wilful, have-it-all-her-own-way dog.

Mainly for Cats

If It's a Him . . .

WALTER – one from Norman Conquest times. Famous mainly for the old Gracie Fields song, 'Walter, Walter, Lead Me to the Altar' and 'The Archers' radio soap serial character, Walter Gabriel. Your cat can restore dignity to the name.

If It's a Her . . .

WINIFRED – after a long-gone saint who soared to fame when, having been beheaded by a rejected princely suitor, no sooner was her head put back in place than she came alive again. That still leaves your Winnie eight lives to go . . .

Names for Dog *or* Cat

WALLACE – could go down better north of the English border, where that bonny fighter William Wallace hae bled for Scotland. Elsewhere in the UK, there's nothing much to stop the name shrinking to Wally, which these days has its own unfortunate meaning. Still, if you feel you've got yourself a rather dozy dog or scatty kitty, why *not* Wally?

WENDY – invented by playwright J.M. Barrie ninety years ago for his play *Peter Pan*. For a fey-looking Maltese or Chihuahua, possibly. Or for a dedicated, home-loving Wendy house-cat.

WILFRED – Old English: there was a St Wilfred over a thousand years ago. You're unlikely to be acquiring a pet with genuinely saintly ways, but Wilfred sounds to us something for an extra-perky dog or cat.

WILLIAM – originally German, though it first hit British shores in the form of W. the Conqueror. After that, over the centuries, came a sprinkling of King Williams. And then, equally famous, Just William, the lovable naughty boy of Richmal Crompton's evergreen stories. If you're getting a puppy, it's odds-on you'll find he's both naughty and lovable, at the start, so William ought to suit him, if you both fancy the name enough.

X

Mainly for Dogs

If It's a Him . . .

XAVIER – Spanish, for a change from all that
Latin and Greek. There was a St Francis Xavier,
patron saint of missionaries, but that's no great
help in choosing a name for your pet. For a
dog, it has a certain not-too-saintly ring to it.

Mainly for Cats

If it's a Her . . .

XANTHE – from the Greek for 'yellow'. Think
of it for your Golden Labrador or Retriever.

For a cat, there's the lovely fawn Burmese/ Siamese.

Names for Dog *or* Cat

XENIA – back to the Greeks for this one. It has to do with hospitality. Neither dog nor cat is going to argue with that (though it's true that Xenia is about *handing out* the hospitality, not sitting there, twitching and quivering, eager to tuck into some of it).

XERXES – was a real live King of Persia, 2,500 years ago. He took on the Greeks in two famous battles. Won one, lost one – then was murdered by one of his own guard. Still, it was a good life, up to then, and Xerxes sounds a real hero.

Y

Mainly for Dogs

If It's a Him . . .

YAPPY – hardly needs explaining, does it?

YIPPY – absolutely no origin that we are aware of, but there are plenty of dogs around that would suit it.

YORICK – he didn't get much of the action in Shakespeare's *Hamlet*, but he made a great Eng. Lit. quote, alas . . . for the kind of dog who looks woeful even when he's opening his birthday presents. Back to the Basset, perhaps.

If It's a Her . . .

YOLANDA – a stray shoot from the pretty flower-name, Violet. This version sounds more suited to eager Actionwoman than fragrant *hausfrau*: Setter, Weimaraner.

Mainly for Cats

If it's a Her . . .

YVETTE – the sort of name that used to fill the character-lists of old French films. Is your cat going to be a cabaret singer, for example? Yvette was absolutely invented for such a personality.

YVONNE – closely connected to Yvette, but more actress or housewife, we feel, than nightclub chanteuse.

Names for Dog *or* Cat

YAMAHA – well, there's the Japanese Spitz, originally from Scandinavia. Or there's the

Japanese Spaniel, a delightful squashy-faced little companion dog (Queen Victoria was presented with one, back in the nineteenth century). For speed fans, regrettably, no Japanese Whippet that we've heard about.

YOKO – do we need to explain this one? She needn't, for our purposes, have any Japanese connection whatever. Just a name to keep in mind, for that moment when desperation strikes.

YO-YO – for a real little comedy turn of a dog or cat. The dog who chases his own tail in ever-diminishing circles round the living-room carpet, the Burmese cat who greets visitors with a series of slow neck-rolling somersaults all down the staircase. *That* kind of Yo-Yo.

Z

Mainly for Dogs

If It's a Him . . .

ZACK – as we say, short version of Zachariah: zippy name for a dog that can stand up for itself (and, if need be, its owner) without being one of the mad-mutt brigade that would charge a speeding fire engine head-on.

ZEBEDEE – OK, so the Bible made him famous as father of no fewer than two Apostles, James and John. But BBC television made him far, far more famous, at least in the UK, with the much-loved puppet dog of 'The Magic

Roundabout' children's show. Zebedee types seem to be any of the little dogs with hair all over their eyes (*see Screen Stars*).

If It's a Her . . .

ZANDRA – from Alexandra (*which see*). In the UK, there's really been just the one, hyper-publicised Zandra, name of Rhodes, business: clothes. Either that warms your cockles, or it absolutely does not.

Mainly for Cats

If It's a Him . . .

ZACHARIAH – good old Bible name and eminently cattable. It sounds quite wise, which won't displease your new pet puss: they're nearly all too clever by half. One of the few names that has an acceptable shortened form: Zack (*but see Mainly for Dogs*).

Names for Dog *or* Cat

ZARA – from the Arabic, meaning 'splendid dawn'. Princess Anne named her daughter Zara, though no doubt this had more to do with Arab horses than Arabic learning. Quite exotic, and could be considered for any of the lean and lovely breeds of dog, or the beautiful, leopard-like Egyptian Mau cat.

ZINNIA – pleasing flower name for a not-too-dainty dog or a never-smelly cat.

ZITA/ZETA – you get quite a social range here: there was an Italian Zita who became patron saint of the servant classes, and there was an Empress Zita of Austria, in the early part of this century. Saint Zita kept her title. The other Zita lost her empire. If you pick this name for any kind of pet, can we please agree one thing? She never, ever gets reduced to *Zit*.

ZOE – in Greek, it means 'life'. A Zoe dog or cat

will be zipping around, whether in a National Park or your very tiny kitchen.

ZULEIKA – from the Persian, implying supreme beauty. Brits heard about the name through the late Max Beerbohm's novel, *Zuleika Dobson*, about rum goings-on at a university involving an impossibly alluring girl (yes, indeed, it was she). For a dog, she has to be one of those sleekly wonderful Salukis, Afghans, Greyhounds or perhaps Rough Collies. For a cat, she just has to look totally beautiful.

Saints and Sinners, Heroes and Heroines

All-time Great Goodies

ALEXANDER – [DOG/CAT] grand old Greek martial/royal name. Best-known holder, of course, was Alexander the Great, back in the late BCs. Just right for any of the big, brave dogs – and little ones, too, as long as they have the courage it takes to be a warrior-King. Also for a Siamese or Burmese cat – or street-fighting moggie.

ALFRED – [DOG] old Anglo-Saxon name meaning 'elf counsel', which sounds more like a pixie mouthpiece than a mighty general. Also of course the name of England's famous cake-burning hero-King. Pretty downmarket name, these days, whether for King or serf. You could use it to bring a glamorous toy Maltese down a peg or two. But it wouldn't be at all fair on any cat.

ANASTASIA – [DOG/CAT] now *here's* a grand name for you. Nothing less than a Duchess of the doggie world is entitled to carry the banner for one of the murdered Russian Czar's noble, tragic daughters. Strictly reserved for the super-sleek Saluki or Borzoi. No Jack Russells need apply. Absolutely right for *any* lady cat.

ANTHONY/ANTONY – [CAT] made famous by Mark Antony who piped up for the assassinated Julius Caesar. Noble enough, historically speaking. But not really a *dog* name, is it? If he's a comical, mischievous sort of dog, you could about call him Antonio (as in the old music-hall ditty, 'Oh, Oh, Antonio ...' which at least rhymes with Bonio). But why not consider Mark's original name? (*see Marcus*).

APHRODITE – [DOG/CAT] ancient Rome's Goddess of Love. A bit over the top, really, so probably better suited to a slightly comic-character pet, or something with a rather severe and haughty look. If a *dog*, a long-haired miniature Dachshund. If a *cat*, a Burmese, which uses an imperious, sinister oriental look to cover a knockabout personality.

ARTHUR – [DOG/CAT] a bit boring nowadays, like Alfred. But once upon a time, in the days of King A. and his Knights, the most exciting name in England. A really noble-looking beast – Bernese Mountain Dog, say – might give it the needed lift, if the name has some special appeal for you (*see also Screen Stars*).

BALTHAZAR – [CAT] very kingly: he was one of the three Magi (Balthazar, Jasper, Melchior) in the Bible. Better for a lordly Siamese, perhaps, than a fat round cuddly kitchen puss.

BARNEY – [DOG] saintly name from the beginnings of Christianity (St Barnabas). But also very matey. Would suit a characterful Kerry

Blue or Irish Terrier. Or one of those Anything Dogs.

BLUEBEARD – [CAT] fearsome, murderous villain of seventeenth-century French tale. For the extra-ruthless alleycat.

BOADICEA – [DOG/CAT] after ferocious British warrior queen who perfected kneecapping by fixing knives to whirling chariot wheels. Purists might try to tell you it's really spelt Boudicca. Take no notice. They weren't around then, either, so what do they know? And Her Majesty almost certainly couldn't write her own name, whichever way. Given her rough, tough, ruthless history, this one could do for Doberman Pinscher, Rottweiler – or the more enthusiastic brand of German Shepherd. Likewise a world-class mouser.

BRIDGET – [DOG/CAT] after Ireland's leading lady saint. Has become a comic-housemaid type of name, so could do for a Yorkshire or Cairn Terrier, or possibly the dear old Basset.

BRUCE – [DOG] surprisingly, it's from Normandy, though the Aussies, bless 'em, have hijacked this heroic Scottish King's name (Robert the Bruce, of incy-wincy spider fame). If you were half-tempted by Barry, this might do instead, as marginally less boring. Any name, of course, is given a lift, if the pet has personality. Not so much for a cat – more for a Rough Collie or Pekinese.

BRUNO – [DOG] means plain 'brown'. So, as with Brandy, just consider the colour. Or honour your pet with the aura of the popular British boxer, Frank B.

BURT – [DOG] as in Lancaster or Reynolds. For the all-male canine: Pug, Staffordshire Bull Terrier.

CAMILLE/CAMILLA – [DOG/CAT] in ancient Greek legend, a warlike queen who could run like lightning and walk on water. Fine for a Greyhound, Whippet or Deerhound – and for a pedigree puss, but make sure she can swim!

CASPAR – [DOG/CAT] adapted from Jasper, another of those three Magi (*see Balthazar*).

Needs a fairly exotic breed to attach itself to:
How about a Borzoi or Saluki? Or a towering
Irish Wolfhound?

CECILIA – [CAT] old Roman, best known as the
name of the patron saint of music. Sounds
best for a particularly dainty, civilised pet.
Not the kind who dumps half a dead dor-
mouse on the table next to your Kelloggs.

CLEOPATRA – [CAT/DOG] can there have
been a more feline female in history than this
Queen of Egypt, who fell asp-over-pyramids
for that Richard Burton in the greatest love
story ever told? Such a name is going to
require a very special cat, and no mistake!
You can give this glorious label, of course, to
any kitten who happens to be cuddled in your
nice warm lap at the moment. But frankly, it
has absolutely *got* to be a right royal,
superbly-spotted Egyptian Mau. *It's a dog?*
Well, anything biggish, slimmish and not too
ruffled-looking. But perhaps cut it down to
Cleo, for a canine.

CLINT – [DOG] well, we'll all know who *your*

image-maker is, won't we? In which case, we'll have a pretty shrewd idea what kind of dog you'll be totin' on that bit of old steel rope. And we shall swiftly cross the road the minute we set eyes on the pair of you.

DAMIAN/DAMIEN – [DOG] from old Greek name Damon - meaning, in essence, 'top dog'. The name Damon has come down through legend in the tale of Damon and Pythias. Damon was up for execution by a notorious dictator, Dionysius. Pythias stood in for him while he went to say goodbye to the folks. To everyone's astonishment, Damon came back to face the music. Not least astonished was Dionysius. He was so impressed, he set both friends free. If your dog is one of the super-loyal breeds, make him a Damon/Damian/Damien.

DIANA – [DOG/CAT] she was a goddess, of course, long before a Diana turned up in the British Royal family. Romans worshipped Diana as goddess of hunting. Think of it for a whole string of big hunting breeds: Bloodhound, Swedish Elkhound, Rhodesian

Ridgeback, Pharaoh Hound, Airedale. Also for the hoitier kind of cat.

DOMINIC – [DOG/CAT] after the saint. Suits a big, strong dog, adds stature to a small cat.

EDITH – [CAT] two saints bore this name, both daughters of long-ago English Kings.

EDMOND – [DOG] Old English, made famous by the unfortunate King Edmund the Martyr, believed to have worked lots of miracles after his spear-riddled corpse was laid to rest in Suffolk, at (where else?) Bury St Edmunds. For the dog with that martyred look: Black and Tan Coonhound, Basset Hound.

EINSTEIN – [DOG] not merely the late, great mathematical genius, but even more important, the dog in the hit movie *Back to the Future*.

ERROL – [DOG] as with Elvis and Elton, there's only one that springs to mind: the long-dead movie swashbuckle-specialist called Flynn. Rhodesian Ridgeback, English Foxhound, Swedish Elkhound.

ESTHER – [CAT] Biblical name: Esther managed to save her Jewish people from slaughter. Not one, perhaps, for the country kitty who keeps bringing half-portions of vole in through the kitchen window. A.k.a. Hetty.

EUPHEMIA – [CAT] name of a saint who suffered rather a lot, a good many centuries back. Another from the Greek, meaning, roughly, 'sweet talk'. Which comes easily to most cats at suppertime. It shortens, sweetly enough, to Effie.

FABIAN – [DOG] noble family name from ancient Rome. Loads of great generals and one saint, who had been Pope before he was martyred, getting on for 2,000 years ago. Ideal for any of the equally noble Great Dane family.

FELICITY – [DOG/CAT] Roman goddess of good luck, followed by several Christian saints. For a particularly sweet-natured pet: a Bedlington Terrier, maybe.

FREYA – [DOG/CAT] she has to be a vision of

sheer beauty, because this was the name of the Norse fertility goddess all the male gods spent their eternal lives trying to get their hands on. Samoyed, Weimaraner, Irish Setter, Saluki, Borzoi, Rough Collie. Or one of the exquisite long-haired pedigree cats.

GARETH – [DOG] Welsh-type hero name invented by the writer Malory 500 years or so ago. For your heroic-but-gentle Giant Schnauzer, Keeshond, or Norfolk/Scottish/Sealyham Terrier. Having picked such a distinguished name, try to prevent it turning into Garry or Gary.

GEORGE – [DOG] is the patron saint of England, and the name has that rock-solid, dependable sound.

GERMAINE – [CAT] French saint of 400 years ago.

GIDEON – [CAT] one the of all-time Hebrew heroes. This name would seem to be strangely suitable either for a cat with great dignity or a cat with none at all (if such exists).

HANNIBAL – [DOG/CAT] fine, strong name, after the Kid from Carthage, 2,000-plus years ago, who persuaded his army elephants to struggle up the Alps and totter down the other side, so that he could give a lot of grief to the Italians. Hannibal the Cannibal (Mr Lecter, villain of the film, *The Silence of the Lambs*) may have taken a little gloss off the name. Or maybe not. It would depend on your pet's personal habits. Remember: with a dog or cat, eating *people* does not make him a cannibal.

HECTOR – [DOG/CAT] Trojan warrior name for a warlike pet. Staffordshire Bull Terrier?

HELOISE/ELOISE – [CAT] tragic lover of scholar Pierre Abelard in twelfth-century France. They wrote each other a lovely class of letter, but it all ended in even more tears. For that rarity, the utterly faithful cat.

ISOLDE – [CAT] tragic heroine of Wagner's

opera *Tristan and Isolde* (*see below*): reserve this
one for a supremely passionate puss.

JASON – [DOG/CAT] from old Greek. It really
means 'one who heals', but we all think of
Jason and his Argonauts, much more exciting
chaps who boldly went where no Argonaut
had gone before, and grabbed the Golden
Fleece. Suits the more eager type of puppy –
a spaniel, certainly. With cats, perhaps to be
considered for the pet you don't quite see as
a Jake.

JUDY – [DOG] pet form of Judith, a great Jewish
Bible-times heroine. But watch her with the
local small wildlife: Judith the Great made *her*
reputation by beheading an enemy general
who fancied her, and who came a bit too
close. Would suit a keen ratter, such as a Jack
Russell, Dandie Dinmont or Norwich Terrier.

JUNO – [DOG/CAT] to the ancient Romans, she
was the goddess with the Women's Interests
portfolio. If a dog, a Great Dane. If a cat, a
queenly White Longhair.

KIRK – [DOG] meaning a church in Scotland, though it was originally a Norse word. If your animal is a Kirk Douglas hero or an adventurous Captain Kirk Star Trekkie, he just might accept it.

LANCE – [DOG] short for love-hungry Lancelot, one of King Arthur's more glam followers. Perfectly dashing name for an Afghan, Borzoi, Saluki, Greyhound, Setter.

MARCUS – [DOG/CAT] grand old bit of noble Roman (Emperor Marcus Aurelius, *et al*). Jolly fine for even a half-noble-looking pooch, and as for cats, most of them seem to rise to an occasion when their personal pride is at stake.

MARTHA – [CAT] Bible character who worked her sandals off for the Lord. This would suit an unusually houseproud puss.

NAPOLEON – [DOG/CAT] Yes, we have put him in the Heroes list because it's a long time since we needed to fear the little Frenchman as a villain. Short but noble: Dachshund,

Corgi, Shih-tzu, Papillon, Silky/Toy/Yorkshire Terrier.

NELSON – [DOG/CAT] fighting name for a bit of a warrior. Irish/Norfolk/Scottish/Sealyham/Welsh Terriers, all noted for their courage. And specially appropriate for any dog resembling our national hero, the one-eyed Admiral, with a single eyepatch.

NOAH – [DOG/CAT] good, strong name that long ago went out of fashion, despite the publicity given to it by the heroic chap who built the Ark. Perhaps for the hard-to-house-train pet who can't seem to get away from the puddles.

ORSON – [DOG] one for film fans and Welles worshippers. Has its roots in Urso, Latin for 'bear'. How about your great big Newfoundland or Mastiff?

PERSEUS – [CAT] son of the goddess Danae, in circumstances only an ancient Greek mythologist could begin to believe. To fulfil a prophecy (well, you can't leave those things unfulfilled, after all), Perseus slew his mum's unpleasant dad. Nothing to do with that sweet little creature you've just fallen for? Just don't say we didn't warn you.

PORTIA – [CAT] for the puss who, like Shakespeare's heroine in *The Merchant of Venice*, could argue and charm her way out of a butcher's meat-safe with a pound of heart and be handed a free sausage for her trouble.

ROLAND – [DOG/CAT] was a brave French fellow, in a saga from the Middle Ages. The name suits a big dog and an oh-well, suit-yourself kind of cat.

RUDOLF – [DOG/CAT] a reminder of Rudolph Valentino, the impossibly romantic silent-movie lover of the twenties. It could get very tiresome every Christmas for the rest of your joint lives, with people thinking yours is named after Rudolph the Red-nosed Rein-deer. Other people's fault, not yours, not his. But still something to bear in mind.

SAMSON – [DOG/CAT] mighty Bible hero who

pulled a temple down. Unless you want to take a rise out of your teeny Peke or Papillon, save this for the biggest, strongest ones. Pit Bull, Tosa, Akita, Giant Schnauzer . . . get the picture? For a cat, on the other hand, we feel it doesn't matter so much about his size, as long he has plenty of character.

SEBASTIAN – [CAT] after a saint from way back who was sentenced to death by arrows because he was a Christian, recovered from his wounds, faced up to his would-be killers once more. And was beaten to death. That's the trouble with saints: they don't often die with their sandals off. All the same, a good name for a proud, brave puss.

TERESA – [CAT] saintly name for the cat who would never do a naughty deed (or at least, never get caught at it). Specially suited, we feel, to a sweet-natured puss with a gentle owner.

TESS – [DOG/CAT] tragic heroine of Thomas Hardy's *Tess of the D'Urbervilles*. Tess is a more flouncy version of Teresa. Probably for a country dog or intellectual's cat.

THADDEUS – [CAT] Biblical name (he was an Apostle, no less). Jokey label for a character cat.

TOWSER – [DOG/CAT] old-established name for a rough, tough mongrel. Or name your cat after Tayside Distillery's company mouser, who killed 30,000 mice, was seen on TV, liked his dram or two of whisky and died March 1987, at a well-pickled twenty-three.

TRISTAN – names don't come much more romantic than Tristan, a great Cornish knight in King Arthur's mystic days who got a bit overheated about his Royal auntie. The tale of Tristan and Isolde (*see above*) became an incredibly romantic Wagner opera. Question: is your new pet a Great Lover? Only time, of course, will tell. But you could at least give him the name to live up to.

ULYSSES – [CAT] the ancient Greek mythical

hero famed for his cunning and persuasive tongue. Know a cat like that?

VENUS – [DOG/CAT] old Rome's Goddess of Love, and probably the most famous, if slightly imperfect, statue on earth. Whether dog or cat, she'll need to grow up majestic, imperious, as well as unutterably, divinely beautiful. Most cats, at least, can manage that.

WINSTON – [DOG/CAT] if a dog, it absolutely has to be a Bulldog, to measure up to the better qualities of the late war hero W. Churchill. A cat had at least better be on the tough side. Cigars optional.

YEHUDI – [DOG/CAT] in honour of a great musician, but before you bestow this name on your pretty little cat, do bear in mind that the man plays the violin, and a cat's feelings are easily hurt. Who could be a Yehudi-class dog? Well, he has to be a bit soulful, hasn't he, if not exactly musical. There's the Shih-tzu, who, at least in puppyhood, is a dead ringer for Beethoven. Soulful? The Dandie Dinmont

Terrier does a beautiful soul-packed gaze, in the right mood.

All-time Big Baddies

ADOLF – originally meant 'noble wolf', but there's only one Adolf likely to spring to most minds. Not a bad thought for a fairly unbalanced, carpet-gnashing Alsatian or Doberman. Or, of course, a miniature Dachshund. A nasty-looking mongrel tomcat could certainly carry it off, especially a black-and-white one with ridiculous Hitlerian moustache.

ALEXIS – [DOG/CAT] from Greek for 'helper' or 'defender'. But the inescapable link with glamorous Alexis of the old 'Dynasty' TV soap opera makes this a dead cert for the slinky beauty of a Rough Collie, or Siamese cat.

CAPONE – [CAT] after we-know-who: strictly for mog who looks meaner than mean – and means it!

CRIPPEN – [DOG/CAT] as murderers go, more notorious than he deserved. The poor chap just wanted a bit of peace and quiet from his garish wife, Belle, slightly overdid the tranx, and forfeited public sympathy by hiding the result under the basement flagstones. For the obsessive bone-burier or skulker.

DRACULA – [DOG] yes, there is even a breed to fit this comedy-chiller name: the Transylvanian Hound, a handsome black-and-tan beast with a sinister, bat-like mask. But would you fancy walking Dracula after sundown?

ELFRIDA – [DOG/CAT] Old English for 'strength of the elves'. A Queen Elfrida of a thousand years ago was a ruthless ruler, generally thought to have arranged the demise of her stepson, Edward the Martyr, to put her own son, Ethelred the Unready, on the throne. Strictly for the pet who runs your family.

FAGIN – [DOG/CAT] the Thief of Thieves in Dickens's *Oliver Twist*. This one should be kept for the dog who can filch the turkey from under your carving knife, or the cat who gets the cream *and* the jug.

IVAN – [DOG] best known for the tyrannical sixteenth-century Russian Czar Ivan, son of Ivan the Great, who went off his rocker in his thirties to such effect that he became forever branded Ivan the Terrible. If you think you may have acquired a little friend who looks like turning into a proper terror, think of Ivan. Could be absolutely any brand of pup . . .

JUDAS [CAT] – if he turns out to be eating and sleeping at six different homes as well as yours . . .

KARLOFF – [CAT] after Boris, the celebrated horror-movie villain. (*We did know a chap who tended a giant spider called Boris in the corner of a room in his house. Haven't heard from him lately . . .*)

LUCRETIA – [CAT] best known for Signora Borgia, of the noted poisoning family. For the moggie with a bit of the Devil in her.

MORIARTY – [CAT] ineffably wicked arch-enemy of Sherlock Holmes. Surely no puss could be as evil as that? Um . . .

PIERREPOINT – [DOG/CAT] after Britain's most famous official executioner: whether he goes in the Baddies or Goodies list depends, of course, on your point of view. A Doberman, killer or not, could carry it off with style.

PLUTO – [DOG/CAT] he was, and for all we know still is, the mythological Greek King of Hades (Hell, to you). It would suit a black, black cat.

RAFFLES – [DOG] as a matter of public moral-ity, we feel obliged to put this fictional burglar in with the Baddies. But he *was* a likeable crook, wasn't he? Think of it for your own rascal.

SALOME – [CAT] after the Biblical belly-dancer who demanded, and got, John the Baptist's head on a salver. If she's a Burmese or Balinese beauty who goes into voluptuous ecstasies around your ankles, demanding nothing less than front end of cod on a plate marked Puss, she's a Salome, all right.

VLAD – [CAT] after the terrible Vlad the Impaler, who put thousands of his loyal subjects to death-by-kebab. For the mog who keeps bringing home small wildlife samples.

Your Top Ten Names
for Pets

What do other people call their pets? Here's the Top Ten of pretty well everything, from an RSPCA survey of 400,000 young pet owners.

Dogs	Cats
1. Ben	1. Sooty
2. Sam	2. Tigger
3. Lady	3. Tiger
4. Max	4. Smokey
5. Sheba	5. Ginger
6. Toby	6. Tom
7. Sally	7. Fluffy
8. Lucy	8. Lucy
9. Bonnie	9. Sam
10. Benji	10. Lucky

Budgies

1. Joey
2. Billy
3. Bluey
4. Bobby
5. Snowy
6. Peter
7. Charlie
8. Magic
9. George
10. Tweety

Gerbils

1. Squeak
2. Jerry
3. Bubble
4. Tom
5. Snowy
6. Bubbles
7. Sooty
8. Sandy
9. Joey
10. Sweep

Guinea Pigs

1. Squeak
2. Ginger
3. Bubbles
4. Patch
5. Snowy
6. Rosie
7. Sooty
8. Sandy
9. Bubble
10. Fluffy

Tortoises

1. Speedy
2. Fred
3. Tommy
4. Toby
5. Terry
6. Timmy
7. Leonardo
8. Tomy
9. Donatello
10. George

Mice

1. Mickey
2. Squeak
3. Jenny
4. Minnie
5. Speedy
6. Bubble
7. Tom
8. George
9. Harry
10. Bill

Hamsters

1. Hammy
2. Honey
3. Harry
4. Fluffy
5. Bubbles
6. Snowy
7. Nibbles
8. Joey
9. Gizmo
10. Henry

Ponies

1. Copper
2. Beauty
3. Bramble
4. Star
5. Misty
6. Lady
7. Amber
8. Snowy
9. Holly
10. Biscuit

— Rabbits —

1. Snowy
2. Thumper
3. Flopsy
4. Sooty
5. Smokey
6. Peter
7. Fluffy
8. Bugsy
9. Roger
10. Blackie

Rats

1. Ratty
2. Roland
3. Splinter
4. Ben
5. Squeak
6. Blackie
7. Rambo
8. Tom
9. Rosie
10. Sooty

Stick Insects

1. Sticky
2. Fred
3. Twiggy
4. Tom
5. George
6. Stick
7. Sam
8. Billy
9. Freddie
10. Charlie

Corgi Family Tree

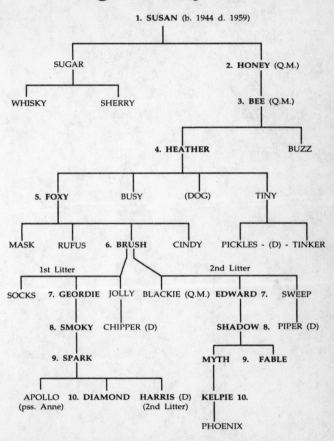

D = Dorgi – the result of mating a Corgi with a miniature
long-haired Dachshund
Numbers – generations in direct descent from Susan

What the Royals Have Called Theirs

The Queen

Her first pet, when she was little Princess Elizabeth, aged seven, in 1933, was a Corgi she called DOOKIE.

Down the years, as well as another Corgi called JANE, the Queen has owned a yellow Labrador named MIMSEY (*all mimsy were the Borogroves*: Lewis Carroll's *Alice Through the Looking Glass*), Mimsey's children, STIFFY and SCRUMMY and a Tibetan Lion Dog, CHOO-CHOO.

But her heart belonged to Corgis. The Corgi, which has been described as having a face like a fox, the rump of a guinea fowl and little bow legs, was first used to drive cattle – because it will bite anything that moves. As footmen and visitors to Buck House can testify.

This seems to have given them more, rather than less, appeal to their fond owner. In 1954, she got SUSAN, who was her loyal companion for the next fifteen years and produced SUGAR, whom the Queen kept, and HONEY, who went to the Queen Mother.

Sugar produced WHISKY and SHERRY. But it was the Queen Mother's Honey who gave birth to BEE, and started today's Buck House lineage. There have been HEATHER and BUZZ, FOXY, BUSY, MASK, RUFUS, BRUSH, CINDY, SOCKS, GEORDIE, JOLLY, BLACKIE (Queen Mother's), EDWARD, SWEEP, SMOKY and SHADOW.

Today's Buckingham Palace Corgi team is FABLE, MYTH, KELPIE, PHOENIX AND PHAROS. Two others, SPARK and DIAMOND, died in 1992.

And then there are the Dorgis . . .

In 1971, the Queen's Corgi, TINY, had seven pups, fathered by Princess Margaret's Dachshund, PUPKIN – a breed put on earth to chase badgers down holes. Today the Queen cherishes

Dorgis called PIPER, HARRIS and BRANDY. But although the Dorgi Dynasty is meticulously recorded at the Palace, the new breed is still refused Kennel Club registration.

In her post-bus-pass years, H M has been persuaded that Corgi Dorgies are not the be-all and end-all. Suddenly, two Springer Spaniels appeared at Buck House: OXO and BISTO.

Prince Philip

As you might expect, for the sportin' Duke of Edinburgh, the only proper dog is a gun dog. His favourite shooting beast is called, imaginatively, RANGER.

Other gun dogs included a dangerously operatic-sounding MIMI, who had a litter of pups named after British cars: FIESTA, LAGONDA, MINX, MINOR. He has also patted black Labradors called after hats – TRILBY, CAP, STETSON, BONNET, TURBAN – and others all starting with D: DRUM, DILYS, DRAMA, DOLPHIN.

Prince Charles

Charles's first official pet, in 1955, when he was six, was a five-month-old Corgi (*what else?*), a Christmas present from the Queen Mother. Princess Anne got one, too. His was WHISKY, hers was SHERRY. The pups' mother was Sugar, father was BUNTER, a.k.a. ROZABEL REBELLION.

But when Charles was just a baby, in 1949, he unofficially appropriated his mother's pet foxhound, SHANDY – a gift from a breeder who heard that Shandy's uncle, RUMMY, had died. (Shandy, of course, had an official pedigree name: SIRAG'S MIGHTY FINE. But even for the Royal family, that was a bit posh to be bellowed out of the back door of Buck House.)

By the age of twenty, Charles decided he didn't really like Corgis. He preferred the more orthodox Labrador. His gun dog, HARVEY, served him faithfully until retiring, aged fourteen, in 1986, with arthritis.

Charles has had two Jack Russells, TIGGER and POOH. Sadly, while he was out with Pooh, a five-year-old bitch, tramping the riverside on the Queen's Scottish estate at Balmoral in April 1994, the dog vanished. Despite the offer of a reward – admittedly, a less-than-heartbroken £30 – she was never seen again.

Pooh's brother – another son of Tigger, born in 1989 – became a Christmas gift from Prince Charles to his dear friend, Mrs Camilla Parker Bowles. Camilla fell in love with the pup, too, and named him FRED – her nickname for the Prince, and one which the English upper classes seem to find a real rib-tickler!

Princess Anne

The Princess Royal has an English Bull Terrier, EGLANTYNE and a Corgi called APOLLO – a gift from the Queen. Her previous dogs have included another Bull Terrier called BP (for Back Pocket, not the oil company: she had a white patch on the left rump of her otherwise chocolate-brown body). Also Gascony Hounds named PLEASURE and RANDOM, a black Labrador, MORIARTY, and a playful Lurcher, LAURA.

Prince Andrew

Gave his bride, the Duchess of York, a Labrador called TARN as a wedding present. In 1988 the Yorks also acquired a terrier called BENDICK – after Fergie's favourite chocolates.

Prince Edward

The Queen's youngest has no dog of his own: possibly he was picked up by the ears once too often by a disciplinarian Dad.

Princess Margaret

Had a Sealyham called JOHNNIE. When the Princess became ill, Johnnie moved in with the Queen Mother at Clarence House and adopted her.

Queen Mother

She has had Corgis HONEY, BEE, BLACKIE and GEORDIE. Blackie, especially, liked the taste of courtier's hand or ankle.

Princess Diana

Sorry, no pet names to report. Reason: no pets. When she was eight, we are told, her beloved guinea pig died. She swore never to have a pet again.

Princess Michael

The only cat person among the Royals. She has had a Siamese called MAGIC. When her Burmese, KITTY, was run over, her husband, Prince Michael, gave her two kittens of the same breed, BESSIE and JESSIE.

Otherwise, as far as Royals are concerned, you can forget cats. There aren't any at Buckingham

Palace. A cat may look at a Queen, but only from the top of the garden wall. And the Queen evidently has absolutely no desire to look at a cat . . .

All Screen Stars, Great and Small

Animals, whether real or cartoon, are always a winner in films and TV series. Here are just some of the screen heroes you could think about (some names, of course, turn up in our other lists . . .)

ALBERT BENJAMIN – red point Persian star of 'Proudfoot'. Kidnapped April 1984, later found dead.

ARTHUR – TV Kattomeat cat.

ASLAN – majestic TV animation lion, in serial also starring a witch and a wardrobe.

BADGER – *Wind in the Willows* fierce hero.

BAGHEERA – black panther in *Jungle Book*.

BALOO – *Jungle Book* big bear.

BAMBI – Disney deer-baby.

BEETHOVEN – St Bernard star of films, *Beethoven* and *Beethoven's Second*.

BENJI – Hollywood movie dog.

BIMBO – Battersea Dogs' Home pet, class of 1980. Brown-and-white mongrel starred in TV film 'Astronauts'. Also starred in TV's 'Just William' and 'The Goodies' and countless commercials. Died 1992, of a stroke, aged ten.

BLACK BEAUTY – horse heroine in films of Anna Sewell novel.

BLACK BOB – Border Collie set up to rival Lassie in Hollywood movies.

BODIE – star of *Steel Magnolias* movie, then TV series as Detective Spot in Toronto.

BUGS BUNNY – cheeky cartoon rabbit.

CEDRIC – TV cartoon dragon.

CHAMPION – the Wonder Horse.

CHARLOTTE – tiny lady spider-authoress at centre of Charlotte's Web, 1970s cartoon movie (*see also WILBUR*).

CHEETAH – one of Tarzan's movie-jungle pals.

CLARENCE – the Crosseyed Lion.

COTTONTAIL – of Beatrix Potter's Flopsy, Mopsy & C. rabbit firm.

DAFFY DUCK – cartoon character.

DIRTY DAWG – homeless, penniless rascal dog in 'Kwickie Koala' cartoon series.

DONALD DUCK – no introduction needed.

DONATELLO – TV Hero Turtle.

DOUGAL – TV 'Magic Roundabout' penwiper dog.

DUKE – Dulux paint-ad Old English Sheepdog, first appeared 1978. Real name Jernard's Likely Lad of Lardams. Replaced by two identical dogs. Died 1991 aged fifteen, leaving 100 offspring.

DUMBO – Disney elephant.

DYNOMUTT – doggy hero of 1970s cartoons.

EEYORE – Winnie the Pooh's mournful donkey.

FELIX – screen cartoon cat.

FERDINAND – brave little cartoon bull.

FLIPPER – TV dolphin.

FLOPSY – see COTTONTAIL.

FRANCIS – Talking Mule in a string of 1950s Donald O'Connor fun movies.

FRISKEY – grey-and-white TV 'Coronation Street' cat, owned by Leeds teenager Paul Rimington.

GARFIELD – famous cartoon cat.

GOLIATH – dog that turns into huge lion, while youthful owner turns into mighty Samson in cartoon series.

GONZO – TV Muppet.

GOOFY – Disney dog veteran.

HEIDI – shaggy Old English Sheepdog: one of the first Dulux dogs, then moved on to Shakespeare.

HENRY – glum Bloodhound in Chunky commercials from 1960s with Sir Clement Freud. Replaced on can labels in 1987 by less suicidal-looking Labrador.

HUCKLEBERRY HOUND – multi-talented movie cartoon dawg.

HUMPHREY – Jack Russell Terrier in 1980s TV series 'All Creatures Great and Small'.

JEMIMA PUDDLEDUCK – ducky B. Potter favourite.

JERRY (of Tom & J.) – cartoon escapologist mouse.

JESS – TV Postman Pat's cat.

KERMIT – the froggy Muppet.

LASSIE – best-loved dog in the world.

LEONARDO – another Hero Turtle.

LUCY – Kate Sugden's Alsatian in TV 'Emmerdale Farm' serial.

MATTHEW – Bulldog shared a rug with a cat and a mouse, peacefully, in Solid Fuel ads.

MAXIMILIAN – TV's Bionic Dog, Bionic Woman Lindsay Wagner's helper. Big superfast Alsatian with four bionic legs, one bionic jaw. Played by dog called Bracken.

MICHELANGELO – yet another Turtle.

MICKEY – don't ask Mickey *Who*!

MINNIE – ditto.

MISS PIGGY – Muppet porker *extraordinaire*.

MITZI-JO – in TV's 'Eldorado' serial, Shih-tzu owned by singer Trish Valentine (actress Polly Perkins, Mitzi-Jo's real-life owner). One of eight dogs, two cats, in Spanish villa.

MOLE/MOLEY – lovable, timid *Wind in the Willows* creature.

MR TOAD – rich, show-off amphibian, friend of Mole.

MRS TIGGYWINKLE – B. Potter hedgehog.

MUFFIN – the TV Mule puppet.

NANNY – Old English Sheepdog, Wendy's minder in *Peter Pan*.

ORVILLE – ventriloquacious TV duck.

PADDINGTON – little lost cartoon bear.

PERKY – TV piglet, with Pinky.

PETER RABBIT – another B. Potter hopster.

PIGLET – Winnie the Pooh small fry.

PINKY – *see PERKY*.

PIPPIN – (see cover) Poodle/Spaniel mix, won top London International Advertising Award. Could earn £1,500 a day. Succeeded by Pippin Junior.

PLUTO – Disney dog.

RADAR – Alsatian hero police dog in bygone BBC TV crime series, 'Softly, Softly'. A real-life guard dog, he could also post letters and bring in the milk. Among the mourners at his funeral were series stars Frank Windsor and Terence Rigby.

RAPHAEL – another Turtle.

RATTY – smooth, sophisticated *Wind in the Willows* riverside rodent.

ROGER RABBIT – cartoon movie hero.

ROLY – TV 'EastEnders' dog: Poodle at Queen Vic pub.

SCOOBY DOO – star dog in Hanna–Barbera cartoons (plus pal Scatty Doo and dim cousin Scooby Dum).

SHERE KHAN – Kipling *Jungle Book* tiger.

SILVER – cowboy Lone Ranger's 'Hi-yo' horse.

SNAGGLEPUSS – permanently panicking cartoon lion.

SNOOPY – warm-puppy hero of 'Peanuts' cartoons.

SNOWY – dog in Tin-Tin cartoons.

SOOTY – TV puppet in kiddie-TV shows.

SWEEP – flop-eared puppet dog in 'Sooty'.

SYLVESTER – cunning cartoon cat.

THUMPER – Disney rabbit in *Bambi* film.

TIDDLES – John Cleese's British Cream cat co-star in Sony video ads. Real name: Karina.

TIMMY – Border Collie starred in TV's 'Famous

Five': real name Toddy. Hard-to-handle dogs' home graduate, adopted by trainers Ben and Joan Woodgate. Died in 1979, a handful to the end.

TOP CAT – cartoon hero.

TOTO – Dorothy's little Cairn Terrier in *Wizard of Oz* movie.

TOWSER – Tayside Distillery company cat, killed 30,000 mice, appeared on TV, liked whisky, died 1987, aged twenty-three.

TRIGGER – Cowboy Roy Rogers' horse.

TWEETIE PIE – the cartoon canary, prey to Sylvester.

WILBUR – celebrated pig in *Charlotte's Web* cartoon movie (*see also* CHARLOTTE).

WILLIE – treasured pet dog of 'EastEnders' old dear, Ethel.

WOODY – movie cartoon Woodpecker.

YOGI – TV cartoon Bear.

Arthur, the Fastest Paw in the West

* For nine years, he was King of the TV Cats. Arthur became famous at the age of six for the

dainty way he scooped Kattomeat out of the dish with his left paw in television commercials.

* Like any human movie star, Arthur went through a court squabble over his contract – about who really owned him. A High Court judge eventually ruled that he belonged to the petfood makers, Spillers.

* Once he was kidnapped from the Essex cattery where he lived, but was found later roaming forty miles away.

* Arthur had his own fan club, signed letters with a paw print, made thirty commercials before retiring in 1975 at fifteen. He died in comfort, a year later. Arthur II, formerly Snowy, belongs to trainer Ann Head.

Lassie and All Her Laddies

Most famous screen pet of all time is Lassie, the Rough Collie (in America, the breed is known as Shetland Collie). So far there have been nearly a dozen Lassie films and over 600 Lassie TV shows.

Lassie's first movie, released in 1943, was

Lassie Come Home, with Roddy McDowell. Elizabeth Taylor, making her first film at the age of eleven, had the bittiest of bit parts. Eventually Liz would become as famous as her doggy leading lady – and Lassie would be dubbed the Elizabeth Taylor of canine movie stars.

In fact, by the mid-1990s, there had been nine Lassies. Every one a gold-plated moneyspinner. And every one played by an all-male Laddie.

Lassie No 1 was a handsome sable-and-white fellow named Pal. He got the job when the Collie originally picked to star refused to dive into a flooded river. Pal starred in seven Lassie movies and died, at the magnificent age of eighteen, in 1958.

Lassie No 2, suitably, was Pal's son, the only one of a long line whose real name *was* Lassie. He worked for six years, then was forced into retirement by cancer, and died aged eight.

Lassie No 3 was the son of Lassie No 2. But the theatrical blood evidently did not run strongly enough in his veins to conquer the embarrassment of playing Leading Lady all the time. In a piece of typical Hollywood ruthlessness, his brother, Baby, was persuaded to snatch the part in mid-movie and become Lassie No 4.

Lassie No 5 was Baby's little boy, murkily named Mire in real life. He did five years on the TV series in the 1960s and lived to be nineteen.

Lassie No 6 was the son of Mire, named Hey Hey!

Lassie No 7 was – *Ho-ho!* - the son of Hey Hey! named, reassuringly for him, in that puzzling world of showbiz, Boy.

Lassie No 8, keeping the grand family theatrical tradition strongly alive, was Boy's boy, quaintly named The Old Man.

And the gorgeous Collie chosen to star in a 1995 follow-up movie called, simply, *Lassie*, is a good-looking young 'lady' called Howard, a direct descendant of all those other female impersonators.

Lassies may come and Lassies may go. But they never, ever, let the title stray out of the family.

The Blue Peter Pet Parade

Bring on the dogs . . .

If ever there was a TV show that tapped into the wellspring of British children's love of animals, it is 'Blue Peter'.

Back in 1962 the producers decided to have a puppy on screen, a pet-substitute for all the children who couldn't have one of their own. That first puppy was an Alsatian-type mongrel bitch. She made her bow in the studio just before Christmas that year, at under two months old.

'Blue Peter' invited viewers to choose a name for her – a tradition followed with the programme's pets ever since. They chose PETRA, feminine of Peter.

In 1965, Petra had eight puppies: CANDY, PETER, KIM, REX, BRUCE, PRINCE, PATCH and ROVER. Seven were given, according to temperament, to children's and old folks' homes, a farm and the army – ROVER became a regimental mascot.

Puppy No 8, PATCH, stayed with Mum in the show. He died, suddenly, at the age of six, in 1971.

He was replaced by a Border Collie named SHEP, who stayed with the programme for seven years.

In 1977, there was sad news for 'Blue Peter' viewers. Their very first TV pet, Petra, increasingly frail at the age of fifteen, had to be put down. A bronze head of her now stands in the 'Blue Peter' garden at the Television Centre, Shepherds Bush, London.

After Shep came GOLDIE, a Golden Retriever who signed on at seven weeks old in May, 1978. When she was nearly three, she had five puppies – four boys and a girl – by a blind people's guide dog called DANNY. By viewers' vote, as ever, the pups were named SANDY, BUSTER, HENRY, PRINCE and LADY DIANA.

Goldie's second litter of eight, fathered by ZEKE, were born in February, 1986. Viewers named them HONEY (after the first in a series of 'Blue Peter' blind people's guide dogs), FERGIE, SNOWY, BRUNO, BONZO, AMBER, HALLEY (after the comet) and BONNIE.

That summer, Goldie retired to a farm in Derbyshire – and daughter Bonnie stepped into the starring role.

In 1991, Bonnie produced *her* first family. There were seven puppies, but one died almost at once. Viewers, once again, were asked to name the surviving six. Forty thousand children sent suggestions. Result: another HONEY, plus BIDDY, LILY, MARGO (after the famous ballerina Fonteyn, who died that year), MAJOR (after

Britain's new Prime Minister, John M.) and TEDDY.

Next, the Cats . . .

'Blue Peter''s first performing puss was a Seal Point Siamese, born early in 1964, who was shown in the studio with his mother, brother and sister when he was only three weeks old. Adopted as a 'Blue Peter' Pet, he was named JASON, by viewer vote. He lived twelve years.

Other 'Blue Peter' cats were twin silver tabbies JACK and JILL, born in 1976. They weren't identical twins, though: Jack had stripes, Jill had spots.

Jill gave birth to kittens, PETER and CHIGGY (after Chigwell, Essex).

An exceptionally beautiful cat, a Balinese Variant – half Blue Point Siamese, half Balinese – was given to 'Blue Peter' in 1986. She was named WILLOW.

. . . And Finally . . .

'Blue Peter' has had two parrot pets, but neither lived long. JOEY, a Brazilian Blue Fronted, died in 1968, of an infection. His feathered successor, BARNERY, also died young, of a lung disease.

The programme also featured tortoises. MAGGIE and JIM joined the staff in 1979, but died together in the fiercely cold winter of 1982, despite the most expert, loving care.

More recently, GEORGE has been the TV Tortoise.

VIPets

* FIVE cats attained the ultimate fame in 1995: they became Royal Mail postage stamps. The five – SOPHIE, ROSIE, KIKKOR, FRED and CHLOE – were pictured in pastel and watercolour by Scottish artist Elizabeth Blackadder. Miss Blackadder, a Royal Academy member, who lives in Edinburgh, included her own three pets in the set.

* BRITAIN'S most important cat, for many years, was WILBERFORCE. He was the No 10 Downing Street cat. Official mouser to the Prime Minister from 1973 to 1987.

* WILBERFORCE was Minister for Mice under

Edward Heath, Harold Wilson, James Callaghan and Margaret Thatcher, and was reckoned to be red-hot at the job, though circumstances precluded his aspiring to the Premiership itself. He retired in 1987 and died the following year.

* IN 1990, a black-and-white tom strolled into No 10 and took up residence and the Mousing portfolio. Staff named him Humphrey.

But what do well-known people call their pets when the dog or cat permits them some sort of say in the matter? Here are some samples . . .

DAVID ASHBY, MP (Leicester NW): ex-Battersea mongrel SAMBA

PADDY ASHDOWN, MP: mongrel LUKE

GEORGE BAKER, TV/movie star: cat SPLODGE

DAVID BLUNKETT, blind Labour frontbench MP, whose guide dog OFFA retired after long and loyal service, now has another Labrador, LUCY

LORD BRENTFORD: yellow Labrador ZARA

FAITH BROWN, TV comedienne: Labrador
    YUSEF

BULLDOG the Wrestler (Davey Boy Smith,
    born Wigan, now living Florida): real
    Bulldog, WINSTON

GEORGE BUSH, US ex-President: MILLIE

BOB CAROLGEES, TV host: Great Dane
    GEMMA (plus former Tiswas show
    puppet, SPIT)

BILL CLINTON, US President: cat SOCKS

MICHAEL COLVIN, MP (Romsey and
    Waterside, Hants): Tibetan Spaniel, COCO

JILLY COOPER, novelist: mongrels GYPSY,
    BARBARA, HERO

KIRK DOUGLAS, veteran movie star:
    Labrador BANSHEE

MICHAEL J. FOX, film star: had a Pit Bull
    called BARNABY, found a new home
    when Michael J. Fox Jnr arrived in 1992

BOB GELDOF, TV/pop star and fund-raiser:
    Yorkshire Terrier GROWLER

LISA GODDARD, actress: Deerhound
ANNIE, mongrel CLARK, Golden
Retriever GERTIE, mongrel GRACIE,
miniature Dachshund FREDERIKA

JOHN ILES, TV actor ('The Bill'): ex-Battersea
mongrel CHIPS

CATHERINE ZETA JONES, actress: Old
English Sheepdog SAM

ROBERT KEY, MP (Salisbury, Wilts) and
government minister: Springer Spaniel,
TIGGER

MICHELLE PFEIFFER, movie star: cat
TRACY

ANGELA RIPPON, TV/radio personality:
Bassett Hound BEN

JOAN RIVERS, US TV entertainer: Yorkshire
Terrier SPIKE

JENNY SEAGROVE, actress: Springer Spaniel
NATASHA

SIR DAVID STEEL, MP (Tweedale-Ettrick-
Lauderdale), Retriever LUCY

ALAN TITCHMARSH, TV gardener: two
  yellow Labradors, GRACE and FAVOUR,
  descended from the Queen's Sandringham
  Kennels

Picking Names at Heartbreak House

EVERY year, London's Battersea Dogs' Home takes in about 17,000 strays and throwouts. When the dogs arrive, many have no known name.

Some are claimed by relieved, delighted owners. Lots are not. And by the time the Great Unclaimed are found new homes, they are no longer the Great Unnamed. But with 250 or so dogs a week needing names, how is it done?

The naming process begins as Mrs Josephine Henderson's staff are assessing each new entrant. Has the dog been ill-treated? Brought up with children? Taught good discipline (as opposed to being thrashed)? Encouraged to play? Been used to just one person?

'The names given often depend more on the mood of our assessors than that of the dog,' Mrs Henderson frankly explains. 'When the assessors are really stuck, they will just reach for the names of supermarkets, beers, any collection that provides an easy list.'

Here is one week's sample, showing that sometimes the name fits, and other times, well . . .

PATCH – white mongrel with black patch on one side of face

DIAMOND – fawn-and-white mongrel bitch

PIPSQUEAK – little black eighteen-month-old bitch with white feet

JUDY – black, tan and cream Alsatian cross, bitch

PENNY – Alsatian cross, around twelve months

CODICE – black-and-tan Doberman

NELLY – Alsatian cross

TRAMP – black-and-tan mongrel bitch, very shy

TOBY – black-and-white male mongrel

MAGPIE – black-and-white Collie type, one
   pink eye

DILEMMA – sable-and-tan Alsatian cross

SANCHEZ – liver, tan and white mongrel

ROBBO'S WORLD – white-and-black
   Greyhound

DINO – Doberman

JASPER – white-and-tan mongrel

FLOP – small, tan-faced mongrel

JERRY – multi-coloured mongrel

FERNANDO – brindle-and-white Greyhound

RAMBO – black-and-white mongrel, one year
   old

MIDNIGHT – black mongrel bitch, aged
   three

RUBY – white-and-tan Whippet

ENA – Doberman

ROSE – fawn Lurcher

PENNY – black mongrel

SPINNER – curly-tailed black-and-tan
   mongrel bitch

LIGHTNING – black-and-tan mongrel bitch

BABY – Staffordshire Bull Terrier cross

OCTAVIA – black-and-tan Alsatian

BASIL – king-sized mongrel

ANDY – confident black mongrel

ARNIE – friendly black-and-white mongrel

CIDER – fawn Alsatian type

CABBAGE – male Doberman

DODO – white-and-tan Labrador cross

ALF – brown-and-sable mongrel

BELSEN and BENSON – two long-stay
  residents: light brown mongrels

LULU – tricolor Rhodesian Ridgeback cross

KANGA – black-and-white Greyhound

NECTAR – tan Alsatian bitch

RUNNER – black-and-white mongrel: *not* one
  for children

ABRAHAM – brindle-and-white Greyhound

The Children's Supplement

Children have a pretty big say in picking a name for the newest pet. We asked a panel of kids – Tania, David, Jane and Daisy – to help out. Here, with absolutely *no* attempt at explaining, is their list, for absolutely *any* pet.

Ariel

Banjo
Bigears
Bilko
Binty
Blinkie
Brasso

Bubbles
Bumper

Carpet
Crystal
Cuddles
Curly
Cutie

Dingdong

Dipper

Dippy

Dozyboots

Dumpling

Dumpy

Fatso

Fatty

Flapper

Flipper

Flopears

Floppy

Flounder

Flowie

Fluff(s)

Frantic

Frostie

Greedy

Grumpy Bumpy

Grunter

Hairy

Icicle

King Pong

Kisser

Kong

Melon

Monster

Muddy

Muffett

Nobby

Orfin

(Orphan!!!)

Peach

Pearl

Periwinkle

Piggy

Podge

Posy/Posie

Puff

Raggsy

Scruffy

Sky

Slobber
Sloppy
Smokey
Snoozer/Snoozie
Snorter/Snorty
Snowball
Snowflake
Snowy
Snuffles
Squeak/Squeaky
Stumpy

Tangerine
Tipp-Ex (*TM)

Topsy
Tricky
Trixie
Twinkle
Twirly

Waffles
Whirly
Wimpy
Winkie
Witch
Wonky
Wuffles
Wumpy

Pets in Matching Sets

Any child lucky enough to be given twin kittens or puppies will have great fun searching for 'together' names. Our gang, with many giggles, came up with the following:

Abbott and Costello

Bangers and Mash
Bill and Ben
Bodie and Doyle
Brandy and Soda
Bread and Butter
Bubble and Squeak
Burger and Beans

Cagney and Lacey
Cannon and Ball
Cheese and Pickle
Chip 'n' Dale
Crisp and Dry
Crunchie and Crackers

Dempsey and Makepeace

Fish and Chips
Flip and Flop

Gilbert and Sullivan

Hammer and Tongs
Holly and Ivy

Kit and Kat

Laurel and Hardy
Law and Order
Lemon and Lime
Lennon and McCartney

Marks and Spencer

Milk and Water

Pepsi and Cola
Pumpkin and Spider

Rag and Bone

Salt and Pepper
Santa and Claus
Snow and Flake
Starsky and Hutch
Sugar and Spice
Sweet and Sour

Whisky and Soda